His Own Words

Claims of Jesus
in the
Gospel of John

by
Harvey Vedder

Publishing Rights Reserved © 2018 by Harvey Vedder. This publication may not be reproduced for publishing without written permission of the Author or Publisher. Non-commercial usage is permitted with credit of this publication as source.

Library of Congress Control Number: 2018906959
Vedder, Harvey 1943−2063
     His Own Words, Claims of Jesus in the Gospel of John / Harvey Vedder
     147 pp. 1 cm
ISBN 978-1-941776-34-6

New England Bible Sales
262 Quaker Road
Sidney, Maine 04330
jptbooks@gmail.com
NewEnglandBibleSales.com
(207) 512-2636

2018
ISBN 978-1-941776-34-6
Publishing rights reserved
by
Harvey Vedder
Harvey@iridologynyc.com

Table of Contents

Chapter	Claims Listed	Page
Preface		**1**
Excerpts		**2**
1	2	3
2	4	3
3	16	3
4	7	6
5	37	7
6	38	13
7	15	29
8	39	35
Pause for Comment		**41**
9	6	61
10	35	64
11	14	76
12	20	80
13	16	88
14	47	93
15	18	110
16	30	120
Pause for Note		**122**
17	(Unenumerated)	133
18	7	133
19	3	137
20	7	138
21	2	141
Closing Comment		**143**

(Total Claims 363)

PREFACE

> "And besides my son, be warned by them:
> Of making many books there is no end, and
> much study is a weariness of the flesh."
> *Solomon, 977 BC*

What you have in your hand is not a book but rather notes by an admirer of Jesus.

When I started to list Jesus' claims like "I am the good shepherd," "I am the light of the world," I expected John's gospel to contain about a dozen. A month later I had over three dozen. My pencil gave way to a spreadsheet and a year of slowly combing pages turned up well over three hundred – a book length list. There were other surprises as well.

No one likes reading lists, myself included. A comment at the side of each quote relieved the repetitiveness, brought context to the content and put exotic claims into ordinary language. Ordinary that is, to a very unordinary man.

Father's Day rolled around this year and my son, a third generation student of John's writings, gifted me a book which he had quietly placed on Amazon as *His Own Words* and there it was, neatly bound into a paperback. My Excel spreadsheet notes are now a book.

Open it anywhere. Meet the man Jesus who was sent to speak the recorded words. Imagine yourself there as listener or in his shoes as someone charged with the impossible task of ambassador from God to man. Find out how ordinary words in heaven become *claims* when spoken on earth. The difficulty you've had understanding Jesus' words may just disappear.

Harvey Vedder, October 2018

Excerpts

Jesus' every communication from the God who sent him is rebuffed by being too incredible to believe or even hold in the mind's eye for more than a couple seconds. This makes his words and sentences claims. Why? Simply because we don't have the ability to believe them! Think about this. The simple statement that God had sent him here as light bounces off like gibberish. Too ethereal. Too wild. Hearers simply toss it out and walk away...but with that little nagging consciousness that *if God really sent a man this is exactly what he would be like.* (p.36)

The king of Israel surely will do as King David and better! The Teacher of Israel will not lapse into the surliness of King Saul. The Way and the Truth and the Life will not be tempted into acting out of character! And his hearers knew it, for they experienced every day that Jesus could not be moved to haste by lack of faith as their scriptures had led them to expect of the Coming One. (*He that believeth shall not make haste.*) Convicted, they (like the court officers who returned without him) have only one rejoinder: *Who are you?* Take that any way you like—sarcasm, attempt to impugn, challenge etc., one is inescapable: honestly blown away by his words, way, speech, gestures, kingly protocol, scathing indictments, intensity, unwavering evenness, they are reduced to naked honesty, *we can't believe someone like you exists.* (p.43)

Among the common people as well as the leadership, he simply could not be dismissed. The fact that they were spoken, have stood for 2000 years, and continue to get identical response from each successive generation, demonstrates their universal applicability over two millennia. No better, or more individual-touching criteria could be devised whereby to gauge humankind's response. I say this to anticipate the question *how can one man's words to a few folks in a small mid-eastern country twenty centuries ago serve to put the entire race of men on trial?* I'll turn that around: How would you do it if you were God, mankind's maker? (p.86)

CLAIM	Chap Verse	COMMENT
...you will be called Cephas	1-42	Authority is asserted when naming a person or object. You don't walk into my house, look at my children, and say "You are Tommie," when I've just introduced him to you as Gerald. Jesus, in renaming Simon Peter is claiming to have authority.
...see angels of God ascending and descending unto [epi] the son of man.	1-51	A claim to 1) exalted status in connection with angels; 2) prophetic fulfilment of Jacob's dream coming to pass on himself.
...mine hour is not yet come.	2-4	A (repeated) claim that he observed and acted on a moral clock superior to chronological clock time.
Fill the watervessels with water.	2-7	A claim that ordinary water can be turned into wine.
My Father's house	2-16	He is claiming 1) God is his father; 2) God has a new name, "Father"; 3) diety, if he is God's son; 4) Solomon's temple really was his Father's house and thus he had rights there as son which no one else could claim.
Destroy this temple, and in three days I will raise it up.	2-19	1) destroy and 2) rebuild (whether the building or his body) both were future claims he would be held to.
Except any one be born anew he cannot see the kingdom of God.	3-3	While not a new claim per se, it explained the words of Ezekiel (36:26) as they had never been explained.
...how, if I say heavenly things to you...	3-12	Claim to be a teacher of heavenly things that even the well-taught teachers of Israel would find difficult to understand. (cf. 6:39)

...thus must the Son of man be lifted up.	3-14	That like Moses' serpent he would be lifted up with similar results—life! This is a claim by Jesus that he would be crucified... a prophecy they had all missed. By saying "thus must" he would have been understood as saying this must happen so that the scriptures be fulfilled.
...every one who believes on him may have life eternal.	3-15	To believe on (Greek *en*, not *eis* here) a person as an act of faith was unprecedented and thus Jesus is claiming he was not an ordinary mortal whom it would be superstition to believe "on." While you can believe a person, believing on a person exalts him to super-human (infallible) status.
God so loved the world...	3-16	He had an intimate knowledge of God unshared by anyone previous to him, enabling him to actually know and tell out God's private feelings!
...that He gave...	3-16	A totally undreamed-of assertion about deity—a god or even God giving in lieu of demanding. Moses' words "because He loved you" in Deut 7 did not penetrate the veil on their hearts to raise the query "is our God more than a perfectly just covenant keeper?"
...his only-begotten Son...	3-16	God had a Son! Not a new thought to pagans, but a son of the gods whose relation to his father was ideal—this was unknown in all their myths. A new and foreign thought to Jewish minds as well, never directly asserted of the God of Israel, and so immediately rejected by conflating to pagan conceptions. Note that while the Rabbins were familiar (see 4:26 below) with the Coming One being a son, none dared put forth the logical query flowing from Ps 110 that perhaps The Blessed (a term signifying Jehovah) had a son! Why did they not ask Jesus "are you telling us God has a Son?"
...whosoever believes on him...	3-16	The Son is to be believed on (eis) ...see 3:15 above. Note this claim substitutes "believe on [him]" for "look on [a brass serpent]" Numbers 21.

...may not perish but have 'zoe aionios'.	3-16	The result of believing on the Son was 1) not perish (an unprecedented claim) and 2) have eternal life. (Again, a claim here connected with believing on a person, a radically new thing. Eternal life previously—at least post-Moses—was solely connected with "keeping them" —the ten commandments) (for example Mat 19:16 ff)
...God has not sent his son into the world that he may judge the world...	3-17	Again, new fact about God as v. 16 above, this time adding another claim that Jesus knew why God sent His son: specifically not to judge but to save (though cf. "for judgment am I come into the world" 9:38)
...but that the world may be saved through him.	3-17	Another new fact about God, that salvation for the world would come through His son (OT references to the salvation of Israel and the world, while specific as to that salvation arising from God through His messiah, yet did not attribute sonship to the Messiah as Jesus announces here).
He that believes on him is not judged...	3-18	Believing on (eis) the son exempts from being judged—another new claim never before made.
...he that believes not has been already judged...	3-18	Nicodemus had never heard heavenly things like this—new fact laid upon fact as Jesus instructs this instructor of Israel. As stated before, a simple fact becomes a "claim" when it exceeds our threshold of belief, as all these heavenly facts did.
...the name of the only-begotten son of God.	3-18	Formal reiteration of v.16 above as a newly claimed title of the one instructing Nicodemus: Only-begotten Son of God. Nicodemus had a lot of rethinking to do on the way home.
...light is come into the world...	3-19	John had said this of Jesus in chapter one, but here Jesus drops it on Nicodemus, making it a claim that he is that "true light."
...and men have loved darkness rather than light...	3-19	Anticipates and answers Nicodemus' unstated question "Why is the world of men condemned?" by claiming to know specifically why God had condemned the world.

...whosoever drinks of the water that I shall give him shall never thirst for ever...	4-14	A bold assertion begging to be tested immediately as it was then and since then for 2000 years!
...but the water which I shall give him shall become in him a fountain of water, springing up into eternal life.	4-14	This claim goes beyond internally affecting just the drinker of Jesus' water. An outflow will, Jesus says, result. Jesus will build on this in a subsequent claim in 7:37, expanding the fountain into a river.
...he whom now thou hast is not thy husband; this thou hast spoken truly.	4-18	Rather than claiming "I can read minds," or, "like Elisha, I can see thoughts," he simply does so without fanfare. Selecting a poignant, impugning fact from her life, he lays it on the conversational table and awaits her response.
I that speak to thee am he.	4-26	Jesus' claim to be the messiah was only made or verified privately to individuals...until Caiaphas slipped up in a public confrontation and Jesus verified his words (not by making the claim himself but) by adducing Caiaphas' own words proclaiming that the awaited Christ (Hebrew messiah) was known to their inner circle as "the Son of the Blessed." (n.b. from Matthew's account the Adjuration (a judicial oath) had just been invoked according to Lev 5:1 and had Jesus remained silent on that occasion, as a witness with information he would have broken the law). Here the claim of Messiahship is spoken as an ordinary response to a sincere statement...if he indeed was the sent one as he claimed, silence would have been inadmissable, and the woman receives the admission.
I have meat to eat of which ye do not know.	4-34	Here Jesus soberly claims and demonstrates that he fed on food which others knew nothing of.

My meat is to do the will of him that sent me	4-34	Ordinary food was for him secondary to a primary food identified vaguely by Moses but never before applied in practice as he was doing—i.e. living directly by words that proceeded from the mouth of God. Deut 8:3. The parabolic significance of giving manna had eluded Moses' audience. Thus Jesus' claim to not only know of, but be quietly living by that mystery food was as incredible as his claim that none of them could convict him of sin.
Go, thy son lives.	4-50	Thus claiming he could heal at a distance.
My Father works hitherto and I work.	5-17	Working together with his Father (whose rest had been broken, making Him a worker since that day) Jesus claims exemption not from the law, but from their traditional interpretation of the Sabbath law. He and his Father are fellow-workers, he claims.
My Father works hitherto and I work.	5-17	Seen by the Jews as a claim on his part that he was equal to God, as a father and a son are equal. By not attributing power to do miracles to God (as req'd by Jewish law of blasphemy) he asserted the truth of their claim…that he was indeed claiming to be God's son.
My Father works hitherto and I work.	5-17	He could and did call *Father*, Him whom they only addressed as God; thus, a claim for being more than a man. Jesus never owned Joseph as his father in words recorded of him, while being "subject to them", both Mary and Joseph as Luke tells us.
The son can do nothing of himself...	5-19	Not a claim that he occasionally was able to imitate God, but ever, consistently and only. This is strengthened in v. 30 by adding "I cannot do anything of myself."
...the Father has affection for the Son...	5-20	A claim that not only did the Father love (Gr: *agapao*) the son (as chap 17) but likes (*phileo*) the son—as one says of a friend. Then he adds a claim as to why, (i.e. because of that liking him) the Father shows him (next claim below)…

...and [the Father] shows him all things which He himself does	5-20	..."all things." This goes beyond other men like Abraham ("Shall I hide from Abraham what I am doing?") who were occasionally shown what He does, to include "all things."
...he will show him greater works than these...	5-20	A claim that even greater works yet would try their wonderment.
...the son also quickens whom he will	5-21	Two claims: 1) he could raise from the dead 2) whoever he chose...not merely whoever God would tell him. Note he does not ask permission to raise Lazarus (11-42) but merely informs Him "on account of the crowd who stand around."
...neither does the Father judge any one...	5-22	A new, heavenly fact never before stated, adding to his "making known" the Father as he had told them he would do, and as Moses had carefully indicated The Prophet that followed him would do as proof of his identity and mission.
...but has given all judgment to the Son	5-22	Jesus thus claims to be officially delegated the judge of all...in lieu of God the Father himself!
...that all may honor the son even as they honor the Father.	5-23	A repeated claim asserting it was the purpose of the Father that all men pay honor to the son. (see 6:29, honor him by believing on him, where believing is called "the work of God")
he that... believes him that has sent me, has 1) life eternal and 2) does not come into judgment...	5-24	Having just (see v. 22) claimed to have judgment given him, he declares in this claim how one may escape that judgment by believing, becoming by that act a possessor of eternal life...
...but is passed out of death into life.	5-24	...and more, such a one will be passed out from under death's domination into "life," something not yet clear, but slowly being opened up in successive claims.
...an hour is coming and now is, when the dead shall hear the voice of the son of God...	5-25	This is about to go from claim to reality at Lazarus' tomb where, as judge of living and dead he demonstrates his claim that individuals or groups hearing his voice while lying dead in their tombs...

...and they that have heard shall live.	5-25	...shall live! And that, not by reincarnation but resurrection (thus settling the Pharisee/Sadducee argument of the afterlife).
...as the Father has life in himself, so He has given to the son to have life in himself	5-26	Thus claiming that the life he possessed as a man was like the life of God the Father himself—a claim no other man had ever made. Claims like this were recognized by Jewish leadership as claims to deity, and forbidden by the law of blasphemy to all but one man: the Son of the Blessed, whom they privately regarded as Deity.
...and has given him authority to execute judgment because he is Son of man.	5-27	A claim that since judgment must be by one's peers—implicit in Moses' dictum *in the mouth of two witnesses or three*—he was uniquely and solely qualified to be judge. The Son of God became our peer when he took on humanity, an enduring act.
...an hour is coming in which all who are in the tombs shall hear his voice...	5-28	This expands v. 25 above to definitively include not just those who willingly hear and live; unwilling as well shall hear that voice. (Whether at the same or different time is not stated here, merely the fact)
...and shall go forth...	5-29	Note, "go forth," not "live," this latter word generally being used only of those receiving life eternal, rather than unending existence in a "resurrection [body] of judgment." (Jesus utters this claim as though anticipating the scene—he speaks, death releases those held, some go forth, others await his next word. Later words from Jesus risen and ascended will distinguish the various spoken commands that accompany the "going forth." For details see 1 Cor 15.)
...those who have practiced good, to resurrection of life...	5-29	These declarations of the newly-announced judge are claims of what he will do with that authority over men. Here in this claim he will raise some to a resurrection of life.
...and those who have practiced evil, to resurrection of judgment.	5-29	Note that life is contrasted with judgment: two distinct forms of resurrection are claimed by Jesus as under his power: raising the "dead in Christ" and raising "the rest of the dead."

(1) I cannot do anything of myself; (2) as I hear, I judge	5-30	Two claims or one? I take (2) to be added to amplify and clarify (1), "Cannot" can be literally "unable, because of limitation" but this neither supports the following nor flows from the immediate context. Rather his mission and his passion as a man had a single focus, to seek the will of his Sender. Thus taking the other meaning "cannot" would mean "I cannot swerve for an instant or all would be lost." What other man (other than perhaps a madman) ever made a claim like this?
...and my judgment is just...	5-30	A judge from his bench might well claim this, but could any add "because I do not seek my will but the will of him that sent me"? I know not of any.
It is another who bears witness of me	5-32	This claim of having witness does not identify who the "another" (Gr: *allos*) is. Possibilities are 1) John Baptist, 2) the Father or 3) the Spirit. If Jesus expected his hearers to know who he was referring to it would doubtless be John, who never witnessed of any one but Jesus. (Note in passing that Jesus spoke each of these claims carefully, considering each separate phrase as he laid it on the table, there to abide unruffled until "the last day" when the words he was speaking would "judge him"—the intended hearer—and every mouth be stopped.) (see 12:48)
...and I know that the witness which he bears concerning me is true.	5-32	Taking the "another" to be John the Baptist, Jesus' claim here would be that he knew John's testimony to be true on other grounds than those his hearers were using: they had said *we do not know* when asked whether John's witness was of heaven, thus rendering "null as to themselves the counsel of God" (Luke 7:30) unlike the people, tax-gatherers and Jesus himself who justified God by receiving John's baptism.

I do not receive witness from man	5-34	Ask, what kind of personage would not welcome credible witness of another man? Only one whose peers were not men would make a claim like this. As though putting teeth in this claim, Jesus adds "but I say this that ye might be saved"—clearly putting them in the class of ordinary men who need salvation, and he in another, more-than-human class.
But I have the witness greater than of John...	5-36	This claim of testimony greater than John's must be from one of his own peers, and Jesus here adduces 1) the works 2) the Father 3) had given him to complete, (works unknown in annals of other gods) these works themselves bore witness such as he could receive, and they could see and witness. Again, note in all these claims and answers the posture Jesus adopts and from which he replies. Jesus ever speaks as a true son of David; while utterly approachable, he is regally removed from the familiarity we presume upon without peers but never with a king.
...the works themselves which I do, bear witness concerning me that the Father has sent me.	5-36	"The Father has sent me" is one of the most repeated claims Jesus makes in John's gospel...at least eighteen occur, not counting equivalent expressions such as "am come."
And the Father who has sent me himself has borne witness concerning me.	5-37	Jesus puts this claim of witnesses to himself and his work third, building the list from what they could not easily deny to things they had no experience identifying. The Father was unknown by name to his hearers except as Jesus spoke of Him, so he patiently keeps repeating this claim of apostleship.
Ye have neither 1) heard his voice at any time, nor 2) have seen his shape/form/ fashion and 3) ye have not his word abiding in you	5-37, 38	Three claims of "knowing all men" (see John's words in 2:24) as well as knowing what knowledge they had at that point of the heavenly claims he was unfolding. By saying they had none, Jesus' implicit claim is that he has indeed. The really wild claim here is that God who is spirit (4:24) (assuming Father and God are coidentified there) has a form or shape!

...they it is who bear witness concerning me	5-39	What other man ever claimed that the holy scriptures of the Jewish nation were written so as to bear testimony to himself? I can think of only one that comes close, a single reference by Paul in Acts 13:47 that would seem to be a claim by Paul that Isaiah 49:6 was fulfilled in his own person. And of course, John Baptist who clearly claimed Isaiah was speaking of him.
I do not receive glory from men	5-41	Not even a little glory? Surely if some man had witnessed Jesus' eyes darting at listeners around him to see if he was being appreciated (as in chap 8 where he fixed his eyes at the ground instead of the woman), or seen him urging someone to speak well of him, or to broadcast his healings, he'd have been sneeringly derided as he doubtless was when asserting (ch 8) *which of you convinces me of sin?* This claim, that he never received glory from men stands uniquely fulfilled in the annals of mankind.
I know you, that you have not the love of God in you.	5-42	This would be an accusation in typical conversation today, and likely provoke denials and an argument: here it does not, why? The shock and surprise of being so easily exposed prevented it. John reports that in their private council they sought to kill him or at least (ch 7) "take him" and shows this was common knowledge among "those of Jerusalem" who unlike the sojourning Jews arriving at Jerusalem for the feast say "Thou hast a demon, who seeks to kill thee?" Thus this claim comes at precisely the proper moment to expose without offering opportunity to argue or casually deny—proof that he not only "knew all [men]" but while knowing did not side with one or the other side but always with God, representing His view.
I am come in my Father's name and ye will not receive me	5-43	Again, a claim of coming just as God had told Moses: *a prophet will I raise up unto them from among their brethren, like unto thee, and will put my words in his mouth and he shall speak unto them all that I shall command him. And it shall come to pass that the man who hearkeneth not unto my words, WHICH HE SHALL SPEAK IN MY NAME, I will require it of him.*

...if another come in his own name, him ye will receive.	5-43	This is an as yet unfulfilled claim reiterated by Paul and elsewhere by John.
...he wrote of me.	5-46	Note that Moses too had anticipated that on hearing his words they would say *Jehovah has not appeared to thee*. God's answer is to give Moses three signs to prove it. Days before his death Moses speaks and pens the words above regarding The Prophet whom Jesus obviously is claiming here as himself.
But if ye do not believe his writings,	5-47	Note that Jesus here claims to know these men better than they knew themselves ...they sincerely thought they believed Moses: Jesus proves they did not.
...the son of man shall give to you [food that abides unto life eternal]	6-27	Here, a claim that the food he would give (like the water he had claimed in chapter four) would feed them more than just diurnally. Has any man ever claimed likewise?
...him has the Father sealed, [even] God.	6-27	This claim, once again of something special God had done to him, must have been understood by his hearers more intelligibly than by me—what is sealing, how and why is it done, by whom and on what occasion? OT references to sealing refer to letters, books, a fountain etc, but never a person. Jesus' claim here takes a well-known action previously only applied to things and says God did it to him.
This is the work of God, that ye believe on him whom He has sent.	6-29	Not only did Jesus not hesitate to speak on God's behalf, telling his questioners exactly what God desired, but refused self-effacing false modesty when that claim involved himself directly. He was the one sent of God, and the only thing worth doing was to believe on him! Who would dare make a claim like this?

It is not Moses who has given you the bread out of heaven, but my father gives you the true bread out of heaven.	6-32	Not only would Jesus dare to put Moses in a lower place than they were wont to place him, but he would claim to be that greater one himself. Any man claiming such a place could lend credence to such an outrageous statement in only one way, by adducing Deut 18 where the lawgiver Moses announces his own demise in the face of a greater one to come. In typical fashion Jesus, conscious of the facts that 1) he *was* the "greater prophet" Moses announced and 2) as such, God would support his claims so he need but state them not defend them!—conscious of this Jesus retains the unruffled calm that would ace a modern lie-detector test. The common men on the street, peers of Jesus, served as the lie-detectors of that day whether parents of a man born blind, visitors to Jerusalem, women, court deputies, a centurion, a fellow crucifixion victim, etc. Even Pilate and Caiaphas could not resist the logic nor the clinching manner in which Jesus delivered his message. I could not maintain that unruffled calm. My injured pride would certainly be haranguing listeners with the fact that I am the great one. Not so Jesus, who merely acted as the great one by serving.
For the bread of God is he who comes down out of (ek) heaven and gives life to the world.	6-33	Considered in isolation from the context, this statement would be regarded as teaching. But if standing there hearing the previous sentences one would discern three claims of Jesus: 1) he in his own person is the bread of God 2) come down out of heaven 3) giving life to the world. Consider, that these would be the words of a madman from whom one simply walks away shaking one's head. Fact: neither the common men nor his detractors and implacable enemies found themselves simply walking away, thus demonstrating that they did not see him as a raving madman.

I am the bread of life	6-35	Note that these words are the answer to the request *give us this bread*, a request he tacitly refused. Thus in disclaiming physical loaves are bread from heaven, his claim to be in his own person the bread of life was a considerate action since the crowd were simple folk, comfortable with things literal more than with metaphor. Having just eaten loaves that came from ??? they would assure themselves of more. He gently turns them away from the merely physical thing given, to himself as the giver. Such kindness backing up such an outlandish claim is consistent with his other claims, for unlike the Jewish leaders whose short-tempered attitude toward the uneducated was "this crowd which knows not the law is accursed!" Jesus' unparalleled patience sets him apart.
...he that comes to me shall never hunger...	6-35	Imagine the disappointment that would follow upon expectantly going up to someone who said these words and being given some put-off. Now ask anyone who has come to Jesus in response to this, "were you disappointed?" and see if Jesus' claim left them flat. At 18 I was hungry, ravenous in fact (ask anyone who knew me in '62) looking for answers, truth, guidance, but after a spiritual encounter with (I believe) Jesus himself while in NYC the following year, that knawing feeling in the pit of my stomach left me. As a matter of fact, the wrenching physical stomach pains I (and my Dad before me) suffered since early teens left, never to return. Hmm...hadn't thought of that for fifty years, glad for this reminder!

...he that believes on me shall never thirst at any time.	6-35	Note Jesus did not drop this claim as bait to attract followers like so many gurus do in 21st century America. He ever spoke words like this in full realization he would be called up by responders bright and simple, learned and ignorant, poor and rich, religious and irreligious. Note too that Jesus puts teeth in this claim by using a strengthened negation, rather than just not or never, so we can't say in response, oh, maybe I misunderstood. And note that unlike Nostradamus or oracles like Delphi there is no intentional ambiguity in Jesus' claims.
Whatever the Father gives me shall come to me	6-37	Okay, what had the Father given him? How can this claim be tested? A few are: those sheep (referring to the disciples and any who subsequently believed on him thru their words), life in himself (5:25), the words he spoke, authority over all flesh—all these and many more are included in what the Father gave him (like Eliezer says of Isaac "unto him has he [Abraham] given all that he has"). This claim is similar to 16:15 "all that the Father has is mine." And note that Jesus believed his own outlandish words, acted on them consistently as though expecting their fulfilment, even when (on only one occasion, Mark 14:36) they failed to materialize. There Jesus asks and receives no answer.
...I am come down from heaven...	6-38	Frequent claim, again prefacing his next one...

...not to do my will but the will of Him that sent me.	6-38	This claim touches indirectly on what is known as "the righteous requirement of the law" a reference to the tenth commandment that forbad, not an action like murder, stealing, adultery etc but the thought itself leading to the action: "Thou shalt not covet" means not even <u>desire</u> in your thought-life. One conclusion surely whispered among those daring souls willing to discuss it was that this tenth command was less than righteous since even God can't require the impossible! Jesus' claim here that he did not practice his own will amounted to throwing down the gauntlet at that tenth commandment in the face of all observers, declaring that he had and would continue to carry out the will of Him who said *Thou shalt not covet*...thus demonstrating that he entertained no thought of unrighteousness with God, but would continue to justify Him in the face of what others regarded as evidence of unrighteousness. The consequences of Jesus' keeping this tenth command by faith in the goodness of God are immense. Note also that there is another, tacit, claim here: that Jesus knew the "will of him that sent me" intimately, and goes on to name two new particulars of that will next.
And this is the will of him that sent me, that of all that He has given me I should lose nothing, but should raise it up in the last day.	6-39	This claim had never been heard before, and thus belongs in the list of "heavenly things" he mentioned to Nicodemus. Once again, a claim no mortal ever thought of, heard, or broached before.
For this is the will of my Father, that every one who sees the son and believes on him, should have life eternal; and I will raise him up at the last day.	6-40	This claim builds on his earlier claims. Since life had been given to the Son, it is up to him how he will use it—to raise from the dead those who came to him believing on him (see 3:14). While the power of those claims was demonstrated in Lazarus, the greater fulfillment of these claims is yet future, when all who are in the grave will respond.

No one can come to me except the Father who has sent me draw him, and I will raise him up in the last day.	6-44	Really two claims here. In the second is another repetition of the claim that he would raise up from the dead, as he had said in the two immediately previous claims. Instead of his hearers replying "Oh, would you please ask the Father to draw me?" their mute silence, as their previous murmuring, closed the door to benefiting from the first claim that coming to Jesus must be preceded by the Father drawing.
Every who has heard from the Father [Himself] and has learned [of Him] comes to me	6-45	In this claim Jesus takes a venerated scripture well-known among them and calmly adds how it would be fulfilled. Isaiah in the words given him, had stated the fact that at the end of days *all thy children will be taught of Jehovah* (taught of God, *Theou,* Jesus says. Coming to Jesus is the result of hearing and learning directly from God the Father—again, a claim no one ever thought of making.
...not that any one has seen the Father...	6-46	Jesus here claims that the divine person whom he had announced as "the Father" was never seen by mortal man.
...he who is of God, he has seen the Father.	6-46	Two claims here: the person John the writer had identified as an only begotten from with (Greek, *para* with gen.) a father, is further identified by Jesus as referring to himself: *of God* in Greek is again *para* with the genitive, denoting immediacy. And per the second claim, this person is the only one among men who has seen the Father. This claim was wildly expanded in 5:37 where Jesus attributes form or shape to the Father, and thus can be 'seen.'

He that believes on me has [laid hold of] life eternal.	6-47	Idiomatically translated by Cassirer as "lays hold" of eternal life rather than simply "has" as KJV, JND, Lamsa etc., this is doubtless closer to how Jesus' actual listeners (as against today's eternal security evangelicals) would have understood it. Nonetheless a strong, repeated claim that directed the Jewish mind away from the course in which their sages had steered them—keeping the law as the only path to life, (broken by the realization that the righteous tenth requirement of the law had never been kept) rather than hoping instead for the lawgiver's promised successor. It is striking to consider in reference to this claim that while the Jewish nation was actively waiting for for The Prophet announced by Moses, they were not anticipating that Moses' successor would be greater than he, and that he would build on the assumption that having learned that lesson they would be in a state of hoping, ready expectation. Those with that hope alive (e.g. Anna, Simeon, Mary, Samaritan woman) were thus being singled out by such claims as this, both by the language in which they were couched, and by the observed behavior of the speaker.
I am the bread of life.	6-48	See 6-35, where this same claim was given in answer to an honest though feeble response of sheep, while here is it their shepherds who, unwilling to step out of the paradigm described in 6-47 above, had murmured drawing Jesus' sharp criticism "murmur not among yourselves." (strange, isn't it that this is precisely what their fathers did to Moses). Instead of listening they now turn up the volume and "contend among themselves" over this repetition of his vexing claim, drawing forth intensified repetitions and additional details they should have known, had they the faith that the sheep demonstrated.

This is the bread which comes down out of heaven…	6-50	Again, a clarification of his previous claims, as an appositive: "this is" etc. As though to say "No, listeners, you did not hear incorrectly; I'll reiterate it until what I say gains entrance to your recall." It is also a Hebraism, as in Ex 6:26 '*this is* that Moses and Aaron,' singling out for attention what might otherwise be missed.
…that one may eat of it, and not die.	6-50	Not only can you eat and gain life and not hunger, but by eating this bread the life one gains will not die (as your fathers died after eating the manna). Note that taking this literally is not expected: Jesus died, the disciples died, Christians have been dying since the beginning, so obviously Jesus meant, and expected believers to take 'not die' in another way. And Scripture written post-Jesus makes a subtle but distinct change, substituting 'fall asleep' when speaking of believers dying unlike the OT expression 'and he died'.
I am 1) the living bread which 2) has come down out of heaven	6-51	Two claims here. Jesus is not merely bread, but living bread. And contrasted with the manna (the bread of the mighty, Psalm 78:25) which was gathered from the ground on which it fell, this bread came down from heaven in another way, and is offered rather than gathered. (As an interesting aside, note the following observations regarding *clustering* in this passage. Clustering is a scribal device lending an intense, emphatic tone to this passage and its claims). Scripture loves clustering the same word in a passage, whether in OT or NT. See for example Exodus 3 where the word "thorn-bush" is clustered five times. Some examples here are: Twenty one uses of the word bread or loaves (Greek *artos*) in this chapter; just three more later in John. 'From heaven' is clustered ten times in chapter six. Flesh (Greek *sarx*) occurs seven times in this passage, five more in the rest of John. Blood occurs six times in John, four are in this chapter six passage. Four of the eight uses of "raise up" in John are again clustered here, as are four of the eleven uses of "will" (Greek *theleema*).

...if any one shall have eaten of this bread he shall live for ever...	6-51	This repetition strengthens the 'not die' claim into live forever. These clarifying repetitions make it utterly impossible to mistake the meaning of Jesus' claim to be that bread.
...but the bread withal which I shall give is my flesh...	6-51	Flesh (as, *in the days of his flesh* Heb 5:7) refers to the condition of being alive in the flesh on earth with life in the blood. When Christians glibly say of Jesus *he gave his life for me* they generally refer to his dying, but it is more, far more. When Paul says in Galatians *who gave himself for me*, "himself" has reference to the life and inheritance that would have been Jesus' sole possession as having finally met the law's claims against mankind, satisfied them, and presented himself at the door to receive the prized blessing: eternal life on earth—the only man ever to come into the good of the law's promise ***the man who shall have done these things shall live by them***. That is, shall live an unbroken life on the earth in a body of flesh and blood. What that life meant to him as the last Adam, the only man ever to taste the joys of unbroken give and take with God, we have little empathy with or understanding of. We rarely quote, and are even puzzled by passages like Ps 102:24 *I said, my God, take me not away in the midst of my days!* Worthy of, and twice offered the kingdoms of this world, Jesus refused them; the third time they will be awarded him in a ceremony detailed in Rev 11. The award comes as a necessary response to the claim he makes here that he would turn down the second offer by refusing the prize (continued life in the flesh) in order to save the world which his God had loved (John 3:16). Thus this claim only serves to darken an already-obscure passage. Western readers are left cold by a man calling himself bread. But Jesus' explanation heightens the inscrutability: bread now is "explained" to be flesh! While "flesh and blood" is readily understandable as the fragile human condition, we can't think beyond it. Jesus does. To "give it" is to embrace death...but Jesus is looking so far beyond death as to be there raising up others from the dead (v. 54). And note, "give," not "give up." Jesus speaks as expecting a transaction, not a cessation of being. Upon giving he will not be gone, but alive in a new condition to receive the reward of giving his humanity, his flesh.

...which I will give for the life of the world.	**6-51**	This claim of what he would do, implies several others. If we start with the scripture Eccl 8:8 *no man hath control over the day of death*, Jesus implies here (and states later) *I have authority to lay it down*, making his claim a direct exception to that rule. Then, if he is to give it, there must be someone who values it and accepts his flesh in exchange for the life of the world. The fact that Jesus knows this and calmly speaks of that transaction amounts to another tacit claim that he, a man on earth, can speak casually of utterly unknown heavenly protocols.

Unless ye shall have eaten the flesh of the son of man and drunk his blood, ye have no life in yourselves.	6-53	Could language be more offensive than this? Even his disciples say "this word is hard; who can hear it?" This extreme claim has never been made by another man; in making it, Jesus seems to be speaking from the posture of confidence in the truth of what he is saying while knowing exactly how offensive it was to all his hearers, friend and foe alike. Only supreme confidence that these were the very words of God could move a man to speak them, announcing as they do, the end of mankind. They stand: soon we will see if God puts His seal on them as two sets of books are opened in the sight of heaven and earth...a book of life where search will be made whether a name stands written or blotted out, and then, books (the second set) opened and "the dead judged out of the things written in the books according to their works." We must wait for God to seal Jesus' claim here by carrying out Jesus' words. Note also that unlike all the prophets who had come before him, Jesus never once proclaims "thus says the Lord" while delivering more solemn words than had ever come from the mouth of a prophet without such preface—a tacit claim to himself be Jehovah. Is silence, like that which greeted this claim, the proper response? Yes, if a madman speaks such outrageous words, but as we have seen the charge of being mad or having a demon never gained credence among Jesus' observers and listeners. Here, an attentive listener ought have asked Jesus what he meant rather than resorting to silence and murmuring!
He that eats my flesh and drinks my blood has life eternal	6-54	For absolute clarity, Jesus restates the negative claim from above in a positive, complementary form and adds…

...and I will raise him up at the last day	6-54	The fourth and last repetition of "I will raise" in this passage, assuring the listener that even if he experienced death after eating and drinking Jesus' flesh and blood, not to fear! Jesus will raise him up again. Note this kind of assurance is exactly what Abraham needed and found regarding his *only one*, and what comforted the hearts of the Thessalonians who were troubled at the passing of some of their number (1 Thes 4:18 and context). Other men have made claims of being able to raise a dead body, but none dares expand the claim to include all who are in the graves as Jesus claimed earlier and unhesitatingly reiterates four times in this passage. To be credible, claims must be stated in unequivocal language, performed publically in the presence of witnesses and be verifiable by later non-witnessing hearers. Compare Jesus' claims to any others, and see whose appear more credible.

...for my flesh is truly food and my blood is truly drink.	6-55	Careful, unequivocal syntax, with equally stressed elements, not "flesh & blood" or "food 'n drink" as we would say in modern, flippant English. Jesus' carefully repeated pronouncements befit the solemnity and dignity of such epochal words, for what we are getting here are the considered, seminal words of the last Adam. Imagine for a moment that you could be there while Adam was nine hundred years old (as, say, Noah's father could and perhaps did) and chat with him. "How did you talk back and forth with God when you came to be, Adam?" "Did you feel strange when you woke and a second being like yourself was there?" "When the mother of all living brought forth a third human, did you feel apprehension? Pride? Wonderment?" Now chat in the same vein with Jesus: "How did you feel as a boy when you directed your attention to fulfilling the law by faith to exonerate God and thereby save the world?" "Were you constantly aware that the fate of the world hung on acceptance of your words, your life, your giving of yourself?" "Did any one of your hearers actually understand when you spoke of eating your flesh and drinking your blood?" "Unlike Adam whose unwitting action forthed an unbroken entail on our race, you broke the entail but then dashed all hopes of the new entail's continuance by quenching that life—how did you feel when you did that?"
He that eats my flesh and drinks my blood dwells in me and I in him.	6-56	Again, a claim no one ever made or would think of making, not impassionedly shouted out by one beside himself, but spoken quietly in the calm, weighed manner of one delivering an essential, life-giving message in such a way that—even if not understood by the actual hearers—would nonetheless burn itself into their minds (and thereby John's pen) at a later time as an occasion presented itself to recall them. This is the way of a true teacher who knows his subject like no other, and is burdened with the necessity of delivering the message in such a way that it will come to mind when required.

As the living Father has (1) sent me and (2) I live on account of the Father, he also who eats me shall (3) live also on account of me.	6-57	Three claims here, the first made previously but with the vital addition here of *living* Father. The second claim is new here and begs explication. One translator comments thusly: "Dia with accusative is not simply by or through...the sense is by reason of what the Father is and his living, or, I live by reason of his being and living." Pause and ask, would a Caiaphas or even John Baptist make such a claim? They had not even acquaintance with the Father sufficient to mouth the words! And claim three asserts that the same will be true of any who—metaphorically, not literally as Roman liturgy teaches—eats Jesus' flesh or more accurately eats *me*. Thus to summarize this section, nine consequences flow from this eating: they would 1) actually eat true bread from heaven unlike manna, 2) be eating from the Father's provenance rather than Moses', 3) never hunger or thirst at any time, 4) eat and not die, 5) live forever, 6) have (ἐχέι, active form) life eternal 7) be raised at the last day, 8) dwell in Jesus and Jesus in him, 9) live on account of me. By any known standard this litany is overload, not comprehensible in ordinary parlance. I can state the fact but am flummoxed by the use of such syntax, other than to speculate that Jesus here as so often is introducing a new syntax consistent with, and needful for, understanding "heavenly things." Ordinary Greek or English rules of grammar are probably inadequate to the subject, mandating the overload.
This is the bread which has come down out of heaven.	6-58	Capstone verse of this "bread" section of John, repeating and summarizing Jesus' unique claim to be the new kind of bread—as the manna was new in its day—but there the similarity ends, as reality replaces the figure, eternal replaces temporal.

...he that eats (lit. masticates) this bread shall live for ever.	6-58	Those eating the manna died! those eating ("masticating" another even more offensively translates it) Jesus would live forever. Thank God for these hard to hear words so unsparingly spoken. I learned as a child that things embarrassing or ridiculous are easily remembered. Here Jesus' intentional offensiveness accomplishes the same...how could anyone not remember them? Thus, stockpiling them with other hard to hear sayings, the mind is filled with a combustible pile that needs only a spark to ignite. To see this in actuality, read the account of Pentecost in Acts 1 where the fiery Holy Spirit torches the tinder!
Does this offend you? If then ye see the Son of man ascending up where he was before?	6-61, 62	This claim was made to his disciples, though probably not simply the twelve as the next verse shows. Note that claims like this set the expectation of the hearer, e.g. as the eleven watched, (Acts 1) Jesus ascended above their heads until a cloud hindered and angels questioned their craned* necks. Peter, still reeling and numbed by the force and number of such altered expectations (Messiah suffering, Messiah more than a man, Messiah approachable yet infinitely distant while on earth, Messiah interested in Gentiles!, Messiah ruling over angels, to name a few) discloses without fanfare or literary excess Jesus' post-cloud whereabouts: *gone into heaven, angels and authorities and powers being subjected to him.* The offensiveness of hearing first-hand such outlandish claims, pales to invisibility as he sees each claim fulfilled. No longer numbed but empowered by tasting, Peter candidly addresses a lame beggar accosting him *what I have I give you...rise up and walk!* Jesus' labored, patient teaching, so ineffectual when delivered, now pays dividends as poor in spirit who have had Isaiah's *glad tidings evangelized* to them forget they are but fisher-folk and step forward in Jesus' footsteps. *(cf. 2 Kings 2:15-18 where observing but unbelieving onlookers were rebuked by Elisha.)

...the words which I have spoken unto you are spirit and are life.	6-63	Since this concept (words being spirit and life) was new to the hearers, it's evident that this is another claim of heavenly things: that is, a fresh view of words familiar but never conjoined before heaven reveals their connectedness. Examples abound as disjointed twos become one. Grace and truth kiss in chapter one, spirit and truth hold hands in chapter four, spirit and life connect here as later way, truth, and life will in the upper room. Something is happening here that transcends what we are noticing as mere linguistic oddities. Heaven has come down to earth visibly, audibly, palpably...the Word began to be flesh, not merely wafting to and fro as a voice in a garden seeking, but tabernacling among us so men could see the glory Moses vainly sought. See John's seasoned reflection on this in the opening of his letter. 1 Jn 1:1-2
But there are some of you who do not believe.	6-64	Finally! a more conventional claim made by many human leaders and would-be leaders, rather than exclusive to Jesus. But instead of warning, threatening or cajoling detractors, Jesus' way is different: he uses the occasion to reiterate and amplify the claim that without the Father drawing men to Jesus, none would come. He is neither bitter nor disheartened by listeners or even close disciples not believing. Compare this with followers of Mohammad who view unbelievers in a vastly harsher way. Once again, the balancedness of this claim—unsparing truth but no rancor—builds credibility in the hearers who do learn to believe.
...no one can come to me unless it be given to him from the Father.	6-65	This claim repeats from earlier but instead of saying "unless the Father who has sent me draw him" the coming to Jesus is a gift rather than the result of active drawing on the Father's part. Such slight differences in Jesus' frequent repetitions clarify and amplify, relieving the author John from making obtrusive editorial comments: Jesus' words, repeated, self-clarify his meaning.

Have not I chosen you the twelve? And of you, one is a devil. (Gr. *diabolos*)	6-70	Clearly a claim rather than an epithet or accusation: Jesus speaks it with authority, not in an outburst but calmly, so as to balance and displace any thought that in so speaking he was boasting of his ability.
My time is not yet come, but your time is always ready.	7-6	A repetition of 2:7, this repeated claim is here made to family members who were offended in him and rebuts acting before his hour. While John as author frequently notes that Jesus did not act because his hour had not yet come, Jesus as well uses the expression to disciples, individuals, crowds and leaders, all of an hour coming or arrived. To some of these he adds "and now is" to presage a demonstration of what had already begun e.g., a lone man Lazarus raised, to be followed by all who are in the graves rising.
...but me it hates, because I bear witness concerning it that its works are evil.	7-7	While claiming to know why one is hated is not unusual, the next claim states the reason as a simple matter of fact, not as an accusation to which he was anticipating denials and counter claims. John notes earlier that Jesus "knew all men", and statements like this demonstrate that knowing.
...my time is not yet fulfilled.	7-8	Again, as 2:4 and 7:6 where he used the word *hour*, he uses *time* here, again claiming he was never in doubt about it, and will not be pushed into men's timeframes, even that of personal family as here.
My doctrine is not mine but that of him who sent me.	7-16	"Sent" again, as in 26 previous claims burning into the minds of hearers that The Prophet whom Jehovah would raise up and send was among them.
If any one desire to practice his will, he shall know concerning the doctrine, whether it is of God, or [that] I speak from myself.	7-17	Thus claiming that understanding of his difficult teaching was possible...provided only that the hearer was bent on changing his ways to those of God, rather than upon hearing to assess or judge the saying and decide on its merit.

...he that seeks the glory of him that sent him, he is true, and unrighteousness is not in him.	**7-18**	Teaching or a personal claim? Both, I think. As a teaching, "seeking another's glory" could be seen in men like Eliezer Abraham's servant, who only sought the glory of his master and master's son. But Jesus is here claiming to be true and be without unrighteousness, a personal claim impossible for even men like Eliezer to make. The corollary claim "he is true" when applied to Jesus, adds to Jesus' claim to be "the truth" (chap 13) a supporting claim to be "true" as well as "the truth."
...no one of you practices the law.	**7-19**	This claim would surely have been challenged but neither Saul of Tarsus, Gamaliel his teacher or any of the scribes and Pharisees hearing Jesus would dare claim to have kept the law. Jesus does, and is unchallenged, even when later his publicly demanded "which of you convinces me of sin?" goes unchallenged. Paul would later say as to the righteousness of the law, that he was "found" blameless i.e., when examined of man's day, but projecting himself into God's day has to confess "what I do not will, this I practice." His own heart condemned him, as he does not hesitate to confess (Rom 7:16), adding that thereby he consented to the [tenth] commandment as more "right" than man's day. Among men, he was found blameless, but they did not see his heart. If likewise challenged Jesus surely could and would have answered that Psalm 119 was true of him: delighting constantly in the law by faith that it came from God, his heart was kept with the result that a man—himself—had finally broken the iron grip in which Law held all other men.

...I am not come of myself...	7-28	The flip side of being sent, is (presuming willingness of the sent one) the actual coming. Jonah was sent, but only came much later. Aboard the ship he could point to himself as sent; but only upon arriving could he point to himself as having come. So building on the edifice of the many "sent" claims here is a testable claim about having come. The living God deals in living realities, and thus was "made flesh" (1:14) to enter into and experience life as His creatures were experiencing it, and so Jesus claims to have come from the One Who "is true," or, (Cassirer trans) the "one who truly *is*."
...there is one who truly *is*...	7-28	Again, familiarity with heavenly things, plus consciousness of "where he came from"—the point of difficulty for the common people in v.27—is the requisite authorization demanded for Jesus to open yet another fact of which they were ignorant: that the Jehovah Moses met at the bush and began addressing by His name JHWH is the only one of whom it can be said that he truly **is. IS-ness** (to coin a new word for the vague and unfamiliar *seity*) belongs to Him alone: all other life exists derivitively from Him. And He, this alone "is-ing" one, Jesus claims as his sender and author of the words he was speaking. I find it numbing to observe the quietly sincere, dignified manner in which Jesus makes—and refuses to defend, other than by another repetition—these many claims. This is his one-hundred fifteenth claim the margin informs me, and reading them one by one as I'm cataloging them here dulls one to the reality of being there and listening to him speak. Not strident, not accompanied by strengthening adjectives others would have added, nor impatient (remember he is generally speaking to sheep in presence of wolves who also get addressed when necessary to defend the sheep.) The lack of substantive replies by those who did have some sense of what he was saying testifies to the gripping power that such words, spoken in such a way, had on the hearers.

I know him... (oida, conscious knowledge)	7-29	Step back and listen from the crowd's perspective: here is an ordinary man saying *God? I know him!* just as we would say—"Peter, oh yes, Jonas' son, I know him well." But no one challenged this man! Why not? Could it be that the hearers were sharply divided as Luke tells us (Luke 12:51 ff) and John later in this chapter beginning at verse 40? Detractors dared not challenge, rulers quietly instructed court officials to apprehend him without causing a ruckus, but united action was not possible until Jesus declares "the hour is come," and the spirit of darkness united all factions to agree with a cry "Crucify!, Crucify!"
...because 1) I am from him and 2) *he* (emphatic) has sent me.	7-29	Note Jesus' observance of formal protocol in these claims, reminiscent of Abraham's dealings with the sons of Heth, Melchisedek or Abimelech — or even Abraham's servant Eliezer with Laban. Unlike those better-advised dignitaries, tawdry leaders rebuff Jesus' ambassadorial overtures delivered according to strict heavenly and earthly protocols. Unruffled by rejection Jesus quietly moves on with the effect John notices as: "They sought therefore to take him; and no one laid his hand upon him, because his hour had not yet come." Serenely confident as Heaven's ambassador, Jesus receives their response: formal rejection of his message. Delivered in the language and dignity of protocol, he can now pause — mission accomplished — and prepare to debrief the One who gave him his charge. Listeners then as readers today uncomprehendingly see only words — and miss observing the end of a litany ongoing since prophets began to speak. *The prophets ended with John.* Jesus closed that litany. Formal rejection of his message *I am from him and he has sent me* is the final act in that drama: "I will require it of him" would now follow as Moses had warned them (Deut 18)

Yet a little while I am with you, and I go to him that has sent me.	7-33	If a chess player preannounced "in the twentieth move, my bishop will checkmate your king," we would watch closely to test his claim of preknowledge or total control of the choreography of the game. Jesus consistently preannounced his movements, a protocol little used among men for obvious lack of knowledge/power/inclination to carry out the preannounced action, but nonetheless a clear demonstration of intimacy with protocols of nobility not familiar to Galileans. Thus I list Jesus' words here as a tacit claim to what he overtly will claim in the next chapter: *I am not of this world.* (and note in passing Jesus' considerateness to his family members: he does not say *I am not of this world* to show them why the world (7:7) hates him—that would have been incomprehensible to his brothers and sisters—but reserves those words for the responsible leaders in 8:23, while simply saying to his family *the world hates me because I testify its works are evil*, words they well understood)
You will be 1) looking for me, but 2) you will not find me. You 3) do not have the means of reaching the place where I am.	7-34	Three conjoined claims that must have been irksome. Jesus predicts his hearers' confusion will increase. He tells them that, actively looking for him they won't have a clue where he is. Then instead of a smug ha-ha, a threat, or even a warning, he terminates the discourse with diplomatic protocol such as Jehovah's sayings by the OT prophets had ingrained his hearers to expect. (e.g. Lev 19 and 20) No explanations, no apologies, no pleading: Jehovah forestalls response by the curt ending "I am Jehovah." Gentile audiences would have found inscrutable Jesus' manner and words here, but falling on ears conditioned by hearing the OT scriptures read out, his Jewish listeners treat them as worthy of consideration, asking "where is he about to go?"

If any one thirst let him come to me and drink.	7-37	Jesus again claims his words will satisfy as water satisfies thirst. But note: Jesus' posture adds a powerful, if tacit, claim. When teaching, Jesus generally sat. But here, like Wisdom (Prov 8 and 9), he stands—a claimant in their temple as she in their streets. "Does not wisdom cry?...she taketh her stand. Beside the gates, at the entry of the city, at the coming in at the doors, she crieth aloud. Unto you men, I call...receive my instruction and not silver, and knowledge rather than choice gold: for wisdom is better than rubies..." By standing to cry out such words, he so identified himself as the coming one that here, as nowhere else in John, the power of that speaking is noted. The crowd asks *is not this the anointed one? the prophet [of whom Moses told us]?* Surprised rulers are convicted by well known scriptures coming to life before their eyes. Powerless, they dispatch their minions who return without taking him, shaking their heads at what they have just seen and heard from this man. Dissension breaks out as one of their own suggests following protocol by hearing from Jesus privately before publicly judging him—to no avail. This speech of Jesus is more than a claim, more than an actor or prophet performing signs: these are not signs but the realities to which previous signs had pointed. The word of God had become flesh and was tabernacling among them, and they found the reality too searching, as their fathers had found Sinai's angel too dreadful. But now they have no Moses to appeal to: *Speak thou with us, and we will hear; but let not God speak with us, lest we die!* Convicted, "every one went to his home, but Jesus went to the Mount of Olives." The drama is over; from this point Jesus no longer is calling the nation to repentence but calling a limited set of that nations' members: "any one who thirsts." And with such he surrounds himself early the next morning.

He that believes on me, as the scripture has said, out of his belly shall flow rivers of living water.	**7-38**	Previous claims had said what water and drinking would do (cf. 6:56) to one who came and believed. Here Jesus' strange claim asserts that such a person will go beyond being a fountain ... rivers of living water will gush from him. Jesus' hearers, mentally searching for something familiar to bring understanding to this unfamiliar reference, would doubtless recall their scribes out-reading strange, mystical words from the prophet Ezekiel: *behold, waters issued out...ran...a thousand cubits...to the ankles...to the knees...to the loins...a river...everything shall live where the river cometh"* Subtle claims like this were the bread and butter of the scribes of Jesus' day.
Neither do I condemn thee: go, and sin no more.	**8-11**	I include this as a claim only because Jesus claims (8:15) to judge no one, and his action here could be seen as judging. In fact, it is surprising that those who walked out did not return later and re-accuse him of making a judgment contrary to Moses' law of stoning. But in that case Jesus need only have had recourse to Hosea 4:14 to show that his "neither do I condemn thee" did not arise from his own heart, but from the scriptures that anticipated just such an occasion. There God announces by Hosea His intent to judge (or rather, *not* to judge) adulterous women; Jesus is merely quoting that judgment, and thus faithful to his claim "I judge no one."

I am the light of the world...	8-12	Imagine saying *I am the light of the world* to close friends, family, people at work. You can't? What if you were delusional or lost touch with reality—okay, most folks agree that's the only way they could say it. What if it were really true, and you were charged with getting it across, demonstrating it, and fielding challenges to it. That is what Jesus is doing here. God wants to interact with his creatures peer to peer. He's too big, too scary, too unfamiliar and beside all that He's a spirit, and we're not sure we believe in what we can't see. God's artless desire to communicate with His creatures encounters a problem—how would you deal with it in His shoes?
...he that follows me 1) shall not walk in darkness but 2) shall have the light of life.	8-12	Jesus' every communication from the God who sent him is rebuffed by being too incredible to believe or even hold in the mind's eye for more than a couple seconds. This makes his words and sentences *claims*. Why? Simply because we don't have the ability to believe them! Think about this. The simple statement that God had sent him here as light bounces off like gibberish. Too ethereal. Too wild. Hearers simply toss it out and walk away...but with that little nagging consciousness that *if God really sent a man this is exactly what he would be like.* Jesus, apparently unperturbed, builds on his statement that he is *the* light —not just *a* light— of the world by challenging anyone to test its truthfulness. 'Follow me' he says, and two things will enter your experience. First, you'll no longer be "in the dark" about anything. Second, you'll never lack having light on your life. Now go and ask anyone who really seems to know Jesus if those two claims have happened to them.

...my witness is true, because I know whence I came and whither I go.	8-14	One common measure of truth (see any dictionary) is "consistency with reality." Philosophy, high on the ladder of human arts, studies the two subjects Jesus mentions—where we come from and where we are headed—a tacit admission it has no idea, else why study to find it? Jesus is here claiming to know the answers, and if true in this, his entire testimony was thus worthy of credence, as indeed the common man was already according him.
...ye know not whence I come and whither I go.	8-14	"You are clueless about my movements" is the sense here given by the present characteristic (rather than time). Note they do not snap back "oh yes, we do," since they really did not have any idea what motivated Jesus: his words hit home. He obviously was not out for money or for power or even for honor—the common motivators of all including themselves—but something else they were not familiar with. Just what did they know about him? First, that he was a loner, that he had companied with the Baptiser and was making more disciples than he, that he had been owned by John as the receiver (and future giver) of God's spirit, had begun doing signs demonstrating power beyond that of the prophets, was unafraid to challenge the leadership by boldly clearing the temple (his father's house, he called it!) of things they knew did not belong there, that his precociousness had surprised Rabbins eighteeen years prior, that he knew letters without being taught in their schools, that he could turn water to wine, was a teacher sent by God and clearly had God with him as one of their leaders confessed early on —and the list goes on. So Jesus points out in this claim that they were reluctant to make any statements about him because they at best were divided on his origin and mission, at worst were clueless and thus any testimony of where Jesus hailed from would lack consistency: "You have no idea where I'm coming from" we would say today.

Ye judge according to flesh...	8-15	This claim could be taken as an outright accusation by the Pharisees. Jesus here continues what he began saying to one of their number: that he had heavenly things to say that they would have difficulty grasping. While claiming to be sitting in Moses' seat as representatives of Jehovah, unlike Moses they were not welcoming the one who came commended by Moses; they feared they might have to give up their "place and [their] nation" if they let Jesus go on. This conclusion was, Jesus points out here, judging "according to flesh."
...I judge no one.	8-15	Jesus had not come to judge the world personally, though of necessity the words he was given to utter were judgmental as no others! No other man had ever come into the world sent of the Father, able thus to speak of what he had seen and heard there.

And if also I judge, my 1) judgment is true, because I am not alone but 2) I and the Father who has sent me	8-16	Any man can and often has claimed *my judgment is true,* but who could add as Jesus here that his words were those of his Father's? Any official wishing to know whether the ambassador addressing him is authorized has but to consult the one who sent him, or examine his papers, his language and manners. All these bear witness whether one is a local fraud posturing as a foreign ambassador, or one whose credentials, manner, habits, and language are those of the country from which he hails. Jesus' manners clearly were of another country, were recognized as such, but were denied official recognition from the leaders of the nation to which he had been sent. This invokes an interesting protocol: what must an ambassador do when his person and message is not received at the proper level by the duly appointed reception committee? For a minor instance of this kind, see David's rebuffed ambassadors in 1 Samuel 10, and note Jesus' related story in Luke 19:12 ff. It is no light matter to rebuff a properly chosen, appointed, outfitted, announced and received messenger—in Jesus' case receiving the gifts the ambassador tendered but refusing the ambassador and his message. The leaders of Israel were doing *despite* not to Jesus alone, but to the God they claimed to honor—the God who would now address the final insult using their own words: "He will miserably destroy those evil men" Mt 21:41. Out of their own mouths Jesus will draw out the judgment, for as he said "I judge no one."

And in your law too it is written that the testimony of two men is true. I am [one] who 1) bear witness concerning myself, and the Father who has sent me 2) bears witness concerning me, 3)...ye know neither me nor my father.	**8-17 and 18**	Picture this scene: a visible man, Jesus, confronts these officials of the Jewish nation, displaying every evidence of credibility and having at his side an invisible companion, no ordinary man or angel but Existence himself: Jehovah means existence. Jesus introduces Jehovah by His up to then unknown name Father and now two men stand there, awaiting acknowledgment. The Pharisees cavil, hedge, derogate and finally ask, not His name but His whereabouts, having refused the credentials already proffered according to protocol. Jesus has at this point repeatedly and formally sought to introduce the Father for acceptance and been ignored. Unofficial acceptance, such as had been tendered at night in private will not satisfy protocol, nor does their current response—asking where this invisible-to-them person is so they can dismissively ignore Him. Jesus' response asserts a claim that the dignity of the One being announced precluded such a slur: the fact that they knew neither himself nor the Father proved they had read neither the letter of recall of the law and prophets, or the letter of appointment and the letter of mission of Law's successor. Upon the witness of two men (here, Jesus and the Father) guilt is established. Jesus closes the conversation leaving them convicted, peeved, but powerless to initiate violence toward him.

Pause for Comment

Pause for a second—the narrative pattern here illustrates why readers get confused, bored or turned off as they read John's gospel. The pattern is: Jesus accosts by making an exotic claim, hearers respond with a question, Jesus answers with a non-sequitur and moves on with no apparent continuity in the dialogue. Here, for example, he claims his witness is true because it is not an unsupported claim of an individual but backed up by his Father. Instead of saying "what do you mean?" his hearers deridingly respond "where is this Father of yours?" to which Jesus replys with a seemingly unrelated "Ye know neither me nor my Father." You as a reader are turned off at this point. The answer you expect is not forthcoming. Jesus defrays the question and turns the conversation to a new and apparently unrelated issue. Instead of answering where his Father is, his answer seems to dodge that issue and meander onto a new issue, whether they know Jesus and his Father. You as a reader see no logic in why Jesus turns the subject rather than answers the question. But a closer look discloses the impeccable logic of Jesus' reply. Conversational etiquette dictates that you answer the original query before moving to a new issue: Jesus is answering the original objection "your witness, as a lone individual is judicially insufficient," with the assertion that the second witness he adduced is there, but *willfully* unknown by them. They knew not the Son nor his Father. Note also, the claim tacit in "your law." I don't say "your coffee" unless to distinguish it from "my coffee." Jesus' reference to "your" law was putting himself outside the class of those who had said to Moses "speak thou with us...but let not God speak with us." He was identifying himself with the lawgiver who went face-to-face with God, rather than the people who "shrank back" from His face.

CLAIM	Chap Verse	COMMENT
If ye had known me, ye would have known also my Father.	8-19	Is this statement a claim or simply repartee? Certainly it qualifies as ordinary back and forth, but Jesus' careful use of words implies more, I'm persuaded. It's not a mere hypothetical possibility, but a calculated invective aimed at their hearts to expose subterfuge. Their scriptures had warned that one who would reply "here am I send me" would also deliver the final sentence—and that one was not Isaiah. "Blind their eyes" would effectively cut them off from hearing and seeing (Jn 9:41), leaving them unconverted and unsaved (Is. 6:10, last phrase). Evangelicals often miss this in pressing grace, forgiveness and being saved. The loosing time for preaching will come to an end. Binding and loosing are companions, just as are joy and sorrow.
I go away, and ye 1) shall seek me, and 2) shall die in your sin; 3) where I go ye cannot come.	8-21	"I go away" is not a claim but is followed by three predictive claims. First, upon Jesus' disappearance, the ones who rejected him (as here) would seek him. His words were credible enough to them that they asked for a guard on his tomb which, while not exactly seeking him, was nonetheless a movement in that direction. Secondly, they would die in their sin, i.e. without turning from the mistake of crucifying their chief. This induration was intensified by turning against Jesus' followers. Thirdly, he repeats his words from 7:34 but instead of saying "ye shall not find me" says "ye shall die in your sin." Instead of saying "where I am" here he says "where I go" (thus making the two coterminous, a frequent teaching habit of Jesus). Thus we have three predictive claims presented here.

Ye are from (ek) beneath, I am from above (ek ton ano)	8-23	Merely an accusation? Tit for tat? From any other man yes; from Jesus, no. The king of Israel surely will do as King David and better! The Teacher of Israel will not lapse into surliness as King Saul. The Way and the Truth and the Life will not be tempted into acting out of character! And they knew it, for they experienced every day that Jesus could not be moved to haste by lack of faith as their scriptures had led them to expect of the Coming One. (*He that believeth shall not make haste.*) Convicted, they (like the court officers who returned without him) have only one rejoinder: *Who are you?* Take that any way you like—sarcasm, attempt to impugn, challenge etc., one is inescapable: honestly blown away by his words, way, speech, gestures, kingly protocol, scathing indictment, intensity, unwavering evenness, they are reduced to naked honesty, *we can't believe someone like you exists*.
Ye are of this world, I am not of this world.	8-23	If someone said this today, we'd think it a claim to be an extraterrestrial thanks to ET, UFO's etc in the media. In Jesus' day such associations were unknown, as was the Christian thought of worldliness. At that juncture the world had never been exposed as a thing opposed to the Father. Thus it was a less-maligned, more neutral thing than we see today, especially in Christian circles. Note that his hearers here don't question this claim as they do his claims connected with the Father. John has carefully prepared us for these claims of Jesus in his prologue, speaking there of the word, the light, the life, the world, its formation, the darkness, the witnesses—all subjects Jesus would take up in order as here. As the announced judge of all, he can preannounce how judgment will flow from his tenure; but as the man amongst men he can in kindness warn of what that claim entails.

I said therefore to you, that ye shall die in your sins.	8-24	Note Jesus' kindness. He has just told them things hard to discourse about: they will die unrepentent in their error, they (unlike him) are from beneath, they are of the world. Now, he offers the reason behind making these statements: he was not of the world and *therefore* should be expected to say such unearthly things. This softens the process for those amongst them like Nicodemus who truly wanted to believe, but found it too much. Jesus' truthing (to make transitive a disempowered English noun) was unsparing; his grace was ever the unexpected, welcome companion to his truth. (technically, not a claim but a reference to another claim. I include it here as a second iteration of that claim)

...for unless ye shall believe that I am (ego eimi) ye shall die in your sins.	8-24	Not a threat, or even a warning per se but a simple statement as you would expect from someone without ulterior motives who arrives from a culture and associations alien to you. The claim here is that he (like Jonah) was sent of God with a societal racial time-bomb. If you were Jesus, charged with communicating the notice of racial destruction (mankind, not merely the Jewish nation) how would you go about it? Your choices today are shouting, grim sign-carrying (like I see on NYC street corners), leaflet distribution, preaching in stadiums, streets, churches etc, hiring a Public Relations agency, or just one-on-one encounters. Think about it in historical terms. Jesus and Jonah did not have the internet or Madison Avenue or global TV. For one man to serve inclusive and proper notice on the entire world involves intricate planning, a retinue of servants, a time schedule, preparation of those receiving the message as well as the one giving it and his chosen witnesses. All this, while observing celestial and terrestrial protocols in the sight of all created beings. The universe-affecting consequences of one man's actions during less than four years is staggering and has only one parallel: Adam's brief tenure unfallen. I repeat, the claim here is that Jesus has squeezed into a single sentence the programme above. I like how another translator renders it: *I have told you already that you will die with your load of sin upon you. Indeed, it is in refusing to believe that I am the one who truly is, that you will die with your load of sin upon you.*

Who art thou? Jesus said to them, Altogether (Την αρχην) that which I also say to you.	8-25	The claim here is *I am what my words portray.* No subterfuge, no lying, no stretching, no embellishment. And on the other hand, discretion, empathy, and passion to please his Father. Priestly language can border on the overly solemn. Prophets' words cry aloud. Ecclesiates' words can be as dry as Proverbs are rich and colorful. Jesus' words deployed all these and more. Precisely. In accord with each circumstance or occasion. John had claimed for Jesus that he was the Word. Jesus proved it. God finally saw his handiwork demonstrated: "the beginning of the creation of God" showed forth a genré of creature, where the life lived and the words spoken were of the same stuff...works and words become interchangeable in Jesus. Thus God was finally able to experience Himself in His creature. Such a first puts this claim in a class by itself. A man had finally tendered to God, offering God opportunity to respond rather than initiate! To appreciate this, simply remind yourself of God's response to his first steward, Adam.
...he that has sent me is true...	8-26	A tacit claim of familiarity with God that enables Jesus to vouch for Him. Unlike flawed pagan gods, He is true. Jesus' claim of being sent into the world rather than being the planned or accidental product of human generation as other men is here again repeated.

...what I have heard from him, these things I say to the world.	8-26	Putting these claims together we get the following. In the nation singled out to await him a man appeared—announced, credentialed, demonstrating words, actions, and previously-unheard facts about the one true God in a manner like no other. He treated men with a dignity and unparalleled kindness, racially reminiscent of God's long-ago visits to Eden abruptly halted by Adam's expulsion. Common people were drawn to this last Adam while the pride of cognoscenti kept such from acknowledging him come on his own recognizance. This resistance by those able to formally, intelligently try his claims is the conflict thread in John's gospel. In the three synoptic gospels the structural element is the 'pericope'—a short narrative account. Not so John. Engagement with the leaders may occur consequent on a pericope, but limitedly. The meat of this gospel is in Jesus' discourses rather than his works. And it is precisely these discourses that present a total enigma to scholar and reader alike. Breaking them into their constitutive elements, the enigma(tic) melts, clarity appears. No longer "claims," we hear ordinary speech of an ordinary man carrying out an extraordinary charge.

When ye shall have lifted up the son of man then ye shall know that I am the one who truly *is*.	**8-28**	Having previously informed the leadership and the people that they would lift him up after rejecting his claims and himself, he can now simply add onto that spoken message by saying "when ye shall have lifted up." Instead of accusingly retorting "*Then* you'll know!" he apprises them of the consequence of ignoring reality: it doesn't go away. Only one who is intimately familiar with such consequences can speak dispassionately of them. This gives us insight into Jesus' projecting himself into the circumstances of rejection, hatred, aloneness that were now just days away, when the son of man would be delivered up into the hands of the gentiles, flogged, spit upon and left on a gibbet to slowly, painfully die a public spectacle. Reality at that point would supravene and bring the full consciousness of who he was. An unearthly characterization and claim, this, to be "the one who truly *is*."
...I do nothing of myself...	**8-28**	Our century has seen actors and impressionists who so seek to portray another that they become that character. But apart from such, the idea of living an entire life expressing another is quite foreign. Jesus is here again claiming that not only is this possible to the human condition, but he was doing it 24/7. God had told humans (Deut 8:3) they could live by every word that proceeded from His mouth, rather than by "bread alone." Jesus is the first one to ever claim to do just that, but with a big difference...(see next comment)

...it is the very things which the Father has taught me that I proclaim.	8-28	Jesus here claims he was not mouthing memorized words, or channeled words (like Edgar Cayce etc) or merely fragments of what he "had heard" but what he had been *taught* by the Father. For this a process was needed: human infancy, childhood and youth spent hearing and learning plus adult reflection on the things learned before proclaiming them in ordinary dialogue. The human condition allows men to be taken over, possessed by other spirits but for a man to willingly, consciously share his body, soul, spirit with God—this was new. Opening up to the God who "is spirit" (John 4:24) and thereby to have the Father intimately "with me" co-experiencing Diety in mortality—this I repeat was new for God and for man. John appears to have grasped this ahead of his fellow disciples and been less affronted than they were. Thus, quite unlike the synoptics, he writes of his experience on Jesus' bosom in such an ordinary, artless style. To John and others like him (e.g. Mary his mother, Mary of Magdala, Nathanael), 'self' had acquired a transient, ethereal, *gifted* quality: a thing to be *used* rather than gratified. And thus the appeal of the "self-less" Jesus to such as these.

And he that has sent me forth is by my side; he has not left me all alone	8-29	Jesus has to tell them the Father is ever by his side! Their scriptures had broadly hinted such a relation between Jehovah and His servant (cf. Is 42 onward, esp passages like 50:4-9). Later he notes their blindness to this fact (I dislike calling this a claim!) by saying: *If I had not done among them the works which no man has done, they had not had sin. But now they have both seen and hated both me and my Father.* We forget the Father was by his side, feeling every slight Jesus experienced, every disdainful glance, every blow from the Roman soldiers, even (I believe) the forsaking Jesus endured of God—*that* was witnessed by the Father in the same manner. Forgetting to notice, we, just like these have to be told again and again by Jesus what is really going on as our unseeing eyes and ears are being pounded with evidences we exclude from our consciousness. Thus when Jesus adduces the reason "because I do always the things that are pleasing to him," it falls on our ears like water on a duck's back.

...because I do always the things that are pleasing to him.	8-29	Imagine a man saying to you "I always please my wife." You might look up to be sure he's not being sarcastic, then test his claim by citing a time he didn't. Religious leaders in Israel never made claims like this for fear of the rejoinder, "Oh, then you are going to live forever and not die?" Jesus said it. Not proudly, boastingly but calmly as a fact they needed to be apprised of since what had become typical among mankind was being treated as normal. Jesus displayed a fresh outlook on what was normal for men. Things like: healing the sick, walking on water, raising the dead, stilling a storm, calling on a colt for royal transport, looking into men's hearts, presuming God to be good without admixture, observing God's rest in lieu of mere shabbat-keeping, doing kindness to just and unjust like God sends rain, loving one's enemies, not lusting, using yea and nay instead of asseverating, keeping the law but not to be deemed righteous, turning the other cheek, multiplying loaves, forgiving both trespasses and sins, honoring prophets—these were ordinary, normal things for men, pleasing to God but far from typical.
...you will know (ginosko) the truth...	8-32	Ask a philosopher how to know the truth—and back off as he expatiates on metaphysics and epistemology or (typically today) tells you there is no such thing as absolute truth. Followers of Jesus test this claim many times a day...have been doing so for over two thousand years. Ask any. They will tell you they found every test they put this claim thru, satisfied. And a claim like this demonstrates either an unusually acute observation ability, or a profound acquaintance with truth itself—a bit heady for a relatively young man in his early thirties.

...and the truth will set you free.	8-32	One of Jesus' most frequently quoted claims today, even quoted by those who would never do so if aware that Jesus said it! Unique credibility accrues when detractors find themselves quoting your words. It would be near impossible to track how many times these words are used today in lectures, motivational speeches and political rants. (Googling the term produces 398,000 hits.)
...me, a man who has spoken the truth to you, which I heard from God	8-40	Passing by verses 33 to 39 as conversational assertions rather than claims, here once again Jesus' claim is that he had direct communication from God and repeated it to these listeners even when repeating it incited attempts on his life. An ordinary messenger or dispatched ambassador faced with such a reaction would surely think twice before repeating the offensive claim. On the American scene, any offensive comment made by a ranking government official quickly draws out a corrective, explanatory apology or retraction and of course the words used are carefully screened in advance to obviate need for apology. Contrast this with Jesus' spontaneous, under-fire statements and ripostes, never added-to, never retracted but on the contrary strengthened by Jesus' assurance that these sayings will endure when heaven and earth passes away and be used in the ensuing day of judgment.

...I came forth from God and am come [from him], for neither am I come of myself, but *he* has sent me.	**8-42**	Note how Jesus locks in meaning by frequently restating negatively a positive statement: *this and not that*. John the writer picks up on, and deploys this exclusion device in the opening words of his gospel, as well as throughout. Later readers Greek or non-Greek might call into question what *coming forth from God* denotes, but with the simple restatement *not come of myself* ambiguity is obviated. Here the claim is not merely of being *sent* as so many times previously but a closely-allied claim is made that, being in God's presence constantly from before Abraham even existed, he had simply *come*, and then adds that that coming was at the behest of God Himself. The first emphasizes *where* he came from and the repetition adds *why*. While oracular in tone, Jesus' statements are clear and definitive rather than mystical and obscure like Nostradamus or the Delphic oracle.
Ye are of the devil as father	**8-44**	a claim to be able to recognize men who were posturing as his disciples, as being imposters fathered by the devil. Lest we think this to be a merely tit-for-tat accusation, Jesus goes on to say things of the devil that suggest he was there in "the beginning" of the devil's activities witnessing what he claims to know here, that *he is a liar and its father*.

...and because I speak the truth, ye do not believe me.	8-45	Having said (v. 43) that they could not understand his speech because they were unable to hear his word, Jesus now goes on to add another reason they could not believe him: those fathered by the devil react to truth as finding something to resist rather than to believe. The next statement, adding a third reason, says this attitude toward truth springs from their parentage—they were not of God, and therefore could not hear the words of God that Jesus spoke. John had said *those who believe on his name...have been born...of God,* (1:12) anticipating Jesus saying it here. Consistent with his claims of being sent from the side of the Father with a message from Him, Jesus never strays or slips (like an imposter or deceived person would) from that posture, addressing them as one who was unearthly while as human as his hearers. This is doubtless the reason for the odd phenomenon we constantly observe in these discourses between Jesus and the Jewish leaders: listening to Jesus they are frozen in the headlight glare like a deer, unable to carry out what otherwise would be their instant reaction.
Which of you convinces me of sin?	8-46	Having just claimed to speak the truth, Jesus now declares himself to be sinless—a claim that goes unchallenged! Have you ever met or heard of a man of whom you could sustain the thought he never sinned? Granted, they had only observed Jesus for a year or two at this point, but surely in that time something would have occurred that a listener could adduce, other than the highly questionable "sin" of healing on the sabbath.

He that is of God hears the words of God	8-47	He claims here to be *speaking* the words of God. They were willing to accord to Moses and the prophets the ability of repeating or writing words of God. Jesus here claims to be speaking them live into their ears, as their fathers had heard in the Sinai interchange between Moses and God "Moses spake, and God answered him by a voice." Interestingly, there they had responded *speak thou with us, and we will hear; but let not God speak with us, lest we die.* Here, they respond "thou art a Samaritan and hast a demon." Note in passing that he here builds quietly on the contrast he had sketched out in 5:47, Moses' writings vs. Jesus' sayings. There is forward movement of Jesus' ambassadorial mission *in spite of lack of understanding or agreement:* while Jesus on occasion does say "as I said to you," he does so far less frequently than we would in comparable circumstances. We "apply more force" where he simply "sharpens the edge," as he doubtless learned as a boy reading Solomon. (see Ec 10:10)
I have not a demon; but I honor my Father	8-49	By replying to their accusation of housing a demon, Jesus' claim to the contrary emphasizes his previous claim that he spoke as directed of God, and thereby fulfilled Adam's mandate to glorify God by being himself and not vitiating that charge by sharing self with a defiled spirit. Note also that not replying to a personal insult (thou art a Samaritan) is consistent with his claim to be an ambassador of good will sent from God: Jesus refuses to be turned aside from his official mission by a personal attack.

I do not seek my own glory; there is he that seeks and judges.	**8-50**	Imagine you flip on your TV and the current American president appears, saying *I never seek my own glory or advantage.* Would you believe him? Or anyone else in the sphere of your acquaintance? Note again that no one challenges Jesus here by saying "Oh yes, you do. I remember yesterday when you..." and citing Jesus doing an action motivated by self interest. Note also that in saying "There is he that seeks and judges" he is claiming to know all about the actors in the drama of divine judgment—consistent with his claim to have come from the Divine, as well as his claim of being sent "not to judge the world." (chap 3)

If anyone shall keep my word, he shall never see death.	8-51	The claim of never seeing death was not lost on Jesus' hearers. Those growing up under the law-teaching of the Pharisees were all their life biting their tongues; it was politically incorrect to ask the question a rich young ruler finally put to Jesus: *good master, having done what shall I inherit eternal life?* None of the Pharisees was observed living forever, while teaching the possibility: *do this and live* as the young Saul doubtless heard from Gamaliel. What we are seeing here is Jesus' inexorable progress in offering the real thing: the Exodus, not from Egypt but from sin. Moses' deliverance of their fathers from Egyptian bondage was only a figure of the real deliverance: bondage to sin. None would admit it. Jesus ignores their caviling ignorance, resuming the thread here of verses 31-36 where his offer of setting them free encountered such resistance that he turned the conversation momentarily away. Just as Abraham's servant Eliezer refused to be sidetracked from his mission, so here Jesus insists they had indeed heard correctly when he showed they were all in bondage without the deliverance he had been sent to offer. This is not a "long rambling discourse without specific direction" as scholars imagine, but a very concise, pointed, logically connected summation. On hearing his claim of having been sent to deliver them, the fathers had had the grace to accept (Ex 4:29-31) Moses' credentials, bow "their heads and worship" ...unlike these proud children three fourteens of generations later. Jesus, as noted, was not sidetracked but had recourse to "Plan B" — the ambassador's sealed instructions in the event of refusal of his message and mission.

...it is my Father who glorifies me	8-54	Deliverance from a more powerful Pharaoh (above) was too much for the leadership. But instead of asking Jesus about this deliverance they mount an ad hominem attack on the messenger. Jesus points out in this claim that as Moses had been drawn out, trained and appointed prior to being exalted in Israel, so the son of man was being glorified by his Father before their eyes after being drawn out of heaven, trained as a man among men, and appointed of God at the bank of Jordan. They are about to find that just as Miriam, Aaron, and Korah were called to answer God for refusing whom He had glorified as leader, so this generation, these leaders, would be called to account for trampling underfoot the Son of God.
And ye know (ginosko) Him not	8-55	A slap in the face! Jesus has been building to this. If I say "you don't know XXXX," it could be a simple assertion. But if you are the world expert on XXXX and someone claims you know nothing of him, your blood pressure would spike. That is what Jesus is doing here. Jesus was carrying out the mission stated in Isaiah 6 and Ezekiel 34. Upon showing them their God, witnessing their rejection of the Father Jesus was displaying, Jesus now states the simple truth in their faces: "You don't know God." Their blood began to boil and minutes later their hands reach for stones to throw.

But I know (oida) him (i.e. intimately) and I keep His word.	8-55	Again, a repetition pertinent to the immediate context of a by now familiar claim to intimate knowledge of God Himself. Here Jesus casually adds *I keep His word,* a claim none of them would dare make publicly lest they be shown false. Moses himself had adjured their fathers solemnly about keeping the words of God by calling them *your life and the length of your days* (Deut 30:20). They understood this to mean that any man who perfectly kept them would live forever — but one by one men died trying. Jesus kept them, was offered the reward of eternal life as a man in the flesh, and (as we'll shortly see) turned it down. Note also that when Jesus here claims to "keep His word" it is *logos*, not the 613 *rhema* they so zealously pursued. Rhema gives the outward form that mouthing a word takes, as against logos including the thought in the heart that gives utterance to words.

Your father Abraham exulted in that he should see my day, and he saw and rejoiced.	**8-56**	Note "your father" not "our father," consistent with the words that follow where, speaking from his undeviating posture as the Jehovah John had announced him to be, Jesus calmly insists on taking the place they should have accorded to him: their Maker, Lord and King. Their tawdry non-acceptance of his claims with greedy acceptance of his gifts fails to turn him aside into untoward, non-kingly language or actions. This single factor explains a host of expressions and otherwise-convoluted discourses that populate John's gospel—to the chagrin of scholars! Pause on that "and he saw and rejoiced." Jesus' claim that Abraham had rejoiced at a mere suggestion prefigured in mystical form (likely at meeting Melchisedec) that the seed he was promised would indeed appear acting in royal, peaceful grandeur—*that* mere foreshadowing made Abraham not merely rejoice but "exult!" Contrast these listeners being face to face with Jesus' veiled grandeur and refusing him! No wonder such steely, judicially-cold words proceed from Jesus toward these his hearers and see-ers as he closes up the book, binds up the testimony and seals the law (Is 8:16) in accord with his ambassadorial instructions (Is 6:8 to 10).

Amen, amen I say unto you, Before Abraham was, I am (ego eimi).	8-58	John Baptist did not need to be told this; born three months before Jesus, John's disciples heard him say of Jesus "he was before me." Scholars may puzzle over why it was needful that Jesus say such provocative words to such an incendiary audience. One clue is that Jesus was the final ambassador in a long succession. By protocol, there cannot be another in that succession; if rebuffed, his charge was to deliver his final indictment. He was, and did. Translating this sentence *before Abraham became, I am* may allow you to hear it as they did. In saying 'ambassadorial instructions' I have reference to Is. 6:8-10 and other scriptures. If you doubt the Isaiah passage is pertinent to this context, you have but to see it quoted in John 12:38 ff, where it appears as John's considered, settled opinion. There is no getting around Jesus' meaning here: by insisting he existed prior to Abraham, he is clearly claiming deity.
Neither has this [man] sinned or his parents, but that the works of God should be manifested in him.	9-3	A fresh claim, not only that Jesus looking into men's hearts could judge of sins as God did, but that he could go beyond the past into what had not yet happened: he could and would shortly use the occasion of blindness to demonstrate the power of God in opening blind eyes (as per Is. 29 and 35 etc). In so speaking, he was at the same time addressing the issue of reincarnation/karma which apparently had gained some credence among the leadership, for the Pharisees shortly will answer the disciples' question *who sinned?* by telling the healed man *you were wholly born in sin,* demonstrating thus their belief that an action prior to this man's birth had rendered him blind in this life.

I must work the works of him that sent me while it is day; night comes, when no one can work.	9-4	When you reply "I'm busy, I don't have time for that," your listener focuses on your motivation. By saying "I must" Jesus is claiming to be motivated by accomplishing his Master's work rather than simply pleasing himself as other men. "Him that sent me" is an iteration by now heard many times. "While it is day" certainly suggested more to the disciples accompanying him than sleeping by night and moving about during the day—by this point they (like the Jewish leaders in 7:35) had gotten the idea that most of his sayings were to be taken allegorically as well as literally. In this last of three claims he builds on the claim of being the light of the world: *day* is where the light is. Night thus becomes the state of their world when he leaves it.
As long as I am in the world, I am [the] light of the world.	9-5	To whom did Jesus say these words, this monstrous claim to be *the* (not *a*) light of the world? To the disciples watching, the crowd around him, the ever-lurking Pharisees, the angelics watching, or as a soliliquy? How about, all the above. Men have only two explanations for Jesus speaking "wierd" words like this—self delusion or clever liar. In the present case they ask how a sane man can unashamedly proclaim himself the greatest light that ever came into the world? The answer is *if he is himself.* Should the sun apologize for being the greatest light in our experience—no, we appreciate it most when it is itself, shining without apology for being the sun. My point here is that Jesus realized that he was the light of the world, rather than hoped or told himself he was. You can blame and censure a man who makes empty claims, but you risk embarrassment when you accuse an Einstein of being a simpleton or Newton a mystic astrologer.

Thou, dost thou believe on the son of man?	9-35	Whether son of man or son of God (the manuscripts vary here) the claim of Jesus to be either or both did not fall on insensitive ears. This man, an unnamed stranger to the world of sight recognizes the voice, the manner, the intonation of this person Jesus and overwhelmed, bows in homage as this time (unlike the first time) he sees (!) the man before him. And note this claim points out a single individual—the son of man—obviously Jesus himself rather than the race of men.
You have both seen him, and he that speaks with thee is he.	9-37	Taking the text of verse 35 to read *son of God*, this would be one of the rare direct claims by Jesus to diety (we'll find another in 10:36 where Jesus quotes himself). The alternate text *son of man,* exalts a man to a status worthy of faith, something incongruent and blasphemous to the ears of Jewish listeners—faith can only be in God himself. But their expectation had been misformed...deliberately it would appear, since when pressed on the issue, the high priest himself readily confessed that the awaited One was indeed *the son of the Blessed.* (see comment on 3:16 and 4:26). Thus either way, whether son *of God* or son *of man*, the conclusion is inescapable: this passage is a claim to diety. You may have to think thru how *son of man* equates to Jesus claiming diety. In brief, while *obedience to a leader* such as Moses or David did not put ordinary men in a worshipped category, putting a man up as an *object of faith* cast a man in a role they should have expected. Jesus was demanding the worship due to God alone by requiring men to *believe on,* rather than to simply *believe* Moses' or David's or Jesus' own words as men set up by God.

For judgment am I come into the world, that they which see not may see, and they which see may become blind.	9-39	Again, this may sound like ordinary discourse but it really is a claim. Here's why. The audience Jesus was addressing were Pharisees, leaders of the most God-honored nation on earth, God's own stewards, and appointed guardians of the revelation He gave Moses fifteen hundred years prior. Jesus used familiar language with them; "judgment" they knew as a thing associated with the "last days" preceding the coming of their Messiah, the judge of all. Thus Jesus was serving formal notice to them that the days were up, he was the judge, and judgment had already begun in the case before them of a man born blind...positive, happy judgment in the case of the blind man, condign judgment in their case.
Verily, verily I say unto you. . . (and full content) . . .I am the door of the sheep.	10-1 to 7	Imagine being confronted by a recent acquaintance who blocks your path and intones: "I am Jack, the beanstalk climber and killer of the giant." Everyone knows the story; no one expects to be accosted by its hero in real life. But that is how Jewish listeners heard the claims Jesus makes here. This man had the incredible nerve to assert to himself, prophesies of David, Jeremiah, Isaiah, Ezekiel and Zechariah, to name a few of the prophet-heroes who had pictured Israel as sheep, God as their owner, and Israel's leaders as shepherds. The figures he uses were familiar from the days of Abraham and history of Moses...*door to the fold, porter, shepherd's voice, lead, follow, [good] shepherd*. John the writer calls these verses an allegory, one they did not understand.

I am the door of the sheep.	10-7	Door of the sheep here is different from verse 2. There his claim was to have gained access to the sheep by presenting himself at the door, *they* gained access by avoiding the door and *mounting up* over the wall. Here he does not enter the door but sets himself between worthless shepherds and the sheep: he *is the* door of the sheep, *they* thieves and robbers—shortly, upon being blinded they will no longer have access to the sheep they pretended to shepherd! (see 11:56 where this begins to be felt by them). They had avoided the first door; he will see to it that any future attempt to get at the sheep would encounter the door—himself!
...if any one enter in by me, he 1) shall be saved and 2) shall go in and 3) shall go out and 4) shall find pasture.	10-9 (4)	Building on the claims to have entered by the proper door, then himself being the door, Jesus now makes two (or really four) fresh claims dependent on these. First, *he shall be saved.* If this sounds vague or even meaningless, ask what the listeners understood by *shall be saved*? The context answers "saved from being blinded." Second, *shall go in and shall go out and shall find pasture.* To appreciate this triple claim, adopt the frame of mind of the recently healed blind man: raptly listening for more of what he'd experienced, while those who cast him out—the unbelieving listeners—would be listening in a retaliatory mode; Jesus had begun taking sheep from their grasp! Instead of being "saved" like the blind man they were being deliberately blinded by Jesus (Is 6:10). The blindness of this man who was born *that the works of God should be manifested in him* would fasten on these men as surely as Naaman's leprosy had settled on profiteering Gehazi, and as Haman's gallows served to hang him.

I am come that they may have life, and have abundantly.	10-10	If you were a prisoner at Auschwitz and one day a man appears, boldly confronts your captors "I've come to release and feed all your prisoners," you can appreciate the awe, shock and disbelief—mingled perhaps with a glimmer of hope—that would thrill your breast. Especially if you had just overheard the lead-in comments upon his reconnaisance inspection accusing them of running, not a workplace as claimed but a torture camp. Jesus' lead-in had been: *all whoever came before me are thieves...the thief comes not but that he may steal, and kill, and destroy. I am come that they might have life!*
I am the good shepherd.	10-11	Note Jesus does not say "a good shepherd," since he was claiming to be a very specific shepherd, the one promised by God in Ezekiel 37:24-5. The implied reference of this claim is to be Jehovah, as their scriptures had foretold: *I will myself feed my flock, and will cause them to lie down, saith the Lord Jehovah.* When approached as a mere man, a teacher among teachers in Israel, with "Good master?" Jesus asks *why do you call me good? There is none good but one, God.* But here, fulfilling Ezekiel's prophesy, he is among them, His flock, as the Lord Jehovah—unquestionably "good," in contrast with the self-serving shepherds who had come before him.

I am the good shepherd	10-14	This expression and the commonly associated image it creates has troubled me all my life. As a child in a small parochial school I was surrounded by captioned pictures of a Jesus figure in long hair, long white robe, stiffly-held crooked staff, placidly looking at a cluster of little lambs with expressionless face. The sheep looked a lot better than the man, in fact almost real. It was comforting to be told at home that artist attempts to paint Jesus were ill-conceived and misguided. While I don't know if my experience was typical, I still shrink back when confronted with any drawing of Jesus as shepherd or otherwise. The expression "Good shepherd" in the mouth of an ordinary man would be a proud empty boast. In Jesus' mouth it takes on an honest life because Jesus' daily work at that juncture consisted of caring for God's sheep, and that not so much because he loved them but because he loved their owner. God's neglected and ill-treated sheep needed more than the perfunctory care the shepherds of Israel were giving...rough handling was so ingrained they had to be plainly told who the good shepherd was! Jesus' claim becomes poignant when you see one such cast-out sheep saying to him: *and who is he Lord, that I may believe on him?* Jesus reveals himself to him, accepts his homage, then turns to the worthless shepherds, calls them thieves and robbers and directs this damaged sheep to look on him as the good shepherd—*after demonstrating in the face of the worthless shepherds that he was indeed of a different sort,* one they could only refer to as *"the good shepherd"* of Ezekiel 34.

...as the Father knows me and I know the Father	10-15	"The Father knows." You are not surprised when a man's disputed claim is finally countered by him invoking "God knows," but for the same man to add "I know God intimately" would get your attention. Even the man who had briefly been to the third heaven would only say at the end of his life "that I may [get to] know him" as something toward which he was headed. Not so Jesus. He calmly announces in this claim that he knew God the Father himself, intimately, as having been with him from the beginning, just as John proclaims in the first verse of this gospel.
...and I lay down my life for the sheep.	10-15	This is both a claim of what he was doing as well as a claim of how he would end that doing. Commenting on the first, the author of *A Shepherd Looks at the 23rd Psalm* details the arduous work a caring shepherd goes thru in the winter and early spring months surveying the mountain paths, the needful resting spots, the quiet watering places, the isolated pasturing spots where he will lead his sheep. It's hard work such as a less-caring shepherd neglects, a "laying down" of one's ease that the sheep may be well cared for. Christians are much more familiar with its second, final sense: *are you willing to forego and give up all claim to your own flock so that I might have a flock such as I desire? Even if it means not having that life that you desire, that "only one" you so dearly love?* and Jesus' response to the Owner of the sheep: *they are thine...I come to thee.*

And I 1) have other sheep which are not of this fold: 2) those also I must bring, and 3) they shall hear my voice; and 4) there shall be one flock, 5) one shepherd.	10-16 (5)	These sound so much like ordinary statements in John's matter-of-fact gospel that the cosmic significance can escape us readers. Up to this point in human history—actually the last two thousand of the four thousand years from Adam—God's stated concern, his official governing activities had all been limited to one nation, one "flock," the descendants of Abraham called Israel! It is a well known, often commented on, rancorous issue among Gentiles and more particularly biblical scholars that from Genesis 12 onward ***the entire "old testament" focuses on one nation***, and Gentiles are all but ignored. After Babel, the nations are given only cursory notice; Israel is everything. Jesus is ending that here. These five statements are being thrown in the face of the Israel leadership; a gauntlet that evoked their murderous response *this is the heir, come let us kill him and the inheritance will be ours.* Note in passing how Jesus goes into detail. An ambassador less bold would limit himself to one terse detail, Jesus confidently uses five. It's like looking a chess master in the eye and saying "after I divest you of both knights, I will capture your queen, force you in a corner and checkmate you in four moves." ...instead of "I hope to beat you."
On this account the Father loves me...	10-17	God loves me! Rather than hearing this as an "in" Jesus had with God the Father, recall that he was charged with the difficult task of introducing Israel to a God whom they supposed to be stern, demanding, distant — rather than loving, kind, sparrow-noting, hairs-of-head numbering, sheep-loving. Thus they had to be plainly told what pleased Him. Men and women using their life energy by laying it down rather than gratifying its whims attracted His attention. Rather than a boast of God loving him, Jesus is teaching them patiently by referencing himself. Thus this claim is to be personally enjoying an intimate knowledge and relationship to an austere Someone they never dreamed of relating to in these ways.

...because I lay down my life that I may take it again.	**10-17** (and 18) (5)	While unusually-motivated individuals might spend their years in self negation, laying their life down for others, Jesus adds something that imparts a uniqueness when he insists he would "take it again." Those men who like Job hoped for resurrection never spoke of that hope with the quiet, almost casual assurance Jesus' claim gives it here. Mankind's wisest, Solomon, concludes no man "has control over the spirit to retain the spirit, and no one has control over the day of death." But Jesus goes on with no less than five intimately connected claims that this scripture, Solomon's dictum, did not apply to him! Here they are: 1) *no one takes it from me* 2) *I lay it down of myself.* 3) *I have authority to lay it down* and 4) *I have authority to take it again.* 5) *I have received this commandment of my Father.* Impossible to mistake his meaning when he (once again, see comment on 8:42) restates, anticipatively meets objections and challenges the listener with a new, related fact. The fact that he could constantly translate into the human idiom, things that were formerly unknown and unknowable to earthbound men provides consistent demonstration of his claim that he was the son of God from heaven.
I told you and you do not believe.	**10-25**	If Jesus' answer to their question *if thou art the Christ, say so to us openly* sounds evasive, it is only because they were being disingenuous asking it. They had already agreed that if he were confessed as the messiah (Greek, christos) they would excommunicate the confessor, and if he himself stated it they would kill him, as indeed happened at his trial. So their question was really a baited challenge. While Jesus' *I told you* is not a claim per se, his statement *you do not believe* was a claim to accurately see the reality their words sought to mask. Jesus *knew all men and had no need that any should testify of man, for himself knew what was in man (*see 2:25). A sincere question is answered, a specious one rebuffed.

...but ye do not believe, for ye are not of my sheep...	10-26 (2)	Two claims here. You do not believe (as above) and *ye are not of my sheep, as I told you.* He had just claimed to know every one of his sheep, calling them by individual names, and now substantiates this claim by telling them they were not among the sheep which his Father had given him.
My sheep hear my voice, and I know them, and they follow me, and I give them life eternal...	10-27	Picture two rival shepherds disputing ownership of a huddle of sheep. One states and demonstrates undeniable evidence that they belong to him: he speaks, the sheep listen and follow him as he walks away from the thieving shepherd. This went on for the entire three seasons of Jesus' calmly separating the common folk of Israel from the false leadership, to their dismay. Here, as they have just watched him seek out the sheep they had driven away (the man formerly blind, now healed) they are stunned to have him throw down another gauntlet: he incredibly states that the eternal life they sought by outwardly keeping the law was not theirs: he not only possessed it, but would give to these scattered sheep the promised reward of his own law-keeping: eternal life!
...and they shall never perish, and no one shall seize them out of my hand.	10-28	This claim is a challenge: try to seize these sheep out of my hand! While they finally succeeded in chapter 18, it was but for a moment as we'll see, and was during the time Jesus calls "your hour, and the power of darkness."
My Father who has given them to me is greater than all...	10-29	Remember before dismissing this as a casual statement, that Jesus is continuing to speak as an ambassador intimate with the sendor, in this case God. They understood from Jesus' frequent use of His new name, Father, that he meant God. They were familiar with Adonai, Elohim, Elyon, Eloah, Shaddai, Jehovah (today referred to as Hashem) El, but to address God by the name Father was **unprecedented prior to Jesus.** Thus each use of this name by Jesus is a claim to knowledge of God they did not possess.

...and no one can seize out of the hand of my Father.	**10-29**	This strengthens the previous claim, that no one could seize the sheep from his own hand, and serves as a very natural lead-in to the next claim.
I and the Father are one.	**10-30**	Isolated from the context of who owns these 'sheep,' i.e., the common people, this claim would seem forced and even more difficult to receive. The context makes clear that the oneness is less that of nature or personhood and more oneness in purpose and action flowing from that personhood...both Son and Father are alike on guard against attempts to steal the sheep, whether for the same or different reasons is not stated, just the fact. The sheer audacity of a human not merely comparing himself to God, but claiming working equality as a peer in planning cosmic activities is unprecedented in my experience, even with madmen. If Jesus had not daily demonstrated actions fully consistent with the claim to be thinking and planning in oneness with God the Father, such a claim would fall flat.

Many good works have I shown you of my Father, for which work of them do ye stone me?	**10-32**	Note Jesus' listeners do not even attempt to reply to the asserted claim of having done many good works: they could not deny them but were unwilling to accept their meaning, thus placing themselves under the ban of Moses! (Deut 18:19) Very carefully Moses had instructed them just before his departure, how to distinguish between a presumptuous prophet's vain words and words of the prophet the Lord would raise up in his stead. So this claim of Jesus to have done good works was indeed verified by the listeners while categorically refused because of his assuming a greater place than Moses. Consider: they knew Moses expected one as great or greater than himself to replace him. They knew the signs and protocols whereby they could identify that one when come. They knew that if ever there was a candidate for being "the prophet," it was Jesus. And they knew Moses had warned of the dire possibility that some would not hear his words, and Jehovah would require it of such a man.

I am son of God	10-36	If we exempt John 9:35 for manuscript authority, and his adjured reply at his trial, then this remains Jesus' sole plainly spoken claim to be the Son of God. Detractors and cults often seek to downplay Jesus' entitlement to being son of God by saying he never actually mouthed the claim, but that others said it of him. Therein lies a strong proof of who he is. One truly a king does not go about pushing that fact in people's faces, but waits and expects their recognition from his kingly bearing, his servants, his words, his largesse, his majesty, his equipage. If Jesus had commonly declared, and encouraged his followers to declare that he was son of God, detractors would be quick to point out the obvious agenda and pride that directed it as being un-Godlike. Mark Twain evidently toyed with this enough to find himself writing a book, The Prince and the Pauper , in which two boys of identical appearance exchange identity, the prince becoming the pauper and the low-life boy taking on the role of the king's son. Mere externals belie, but cannot expunge, internal reality. Nowhere is this demonstrated like in Jesus.
If I do not the works of my Father...	10-37	Another casual reference to God as his father, resting on previous claims and their non-refutal by his listeners.

...believe the works, that ye may know that the Father is in me...	10-38	Here Jesus claims that 1) the Father, God, is in him and 2) that the works done before their eyes were precisely the demonstration of his being truly *the prophet* of whom Moses spoke, as Moses' works done before the eyes of the elders of Israel demonstrated that he was sent of *I AM*, the new name he introduced for Adonai. The lack of refutal by Jesus' listeners is mute testimony to Nicodemas' artless confession *we know that thou art a teacher come from God, for no one can do the works which thou doest unless God be with him.* By saying "we know" Nicodemus is acknowledging that Pharisees knew, but were unwilling to state that Jesus' works proved his identity as *of God.* By coming at night with that honest difficulty, he began to exempt himself as we'll note in two later occasions.
...and I in him.	10-38	I list this out separately as a claim standing independent of the claim "the Father is in me." Any human may claim (and many do) "God is in me," but the claim here says that in the same way that Jesus allowed the Father access to himself, so the Father allowed Jesus access to Himself. They were "men of the same protocol," unlike the run of men who claim that God is in them—such do not dare make the claim that they are (as something desired or needed) in Him. Note that Jesus spoke these same words to Philip in reply to *Lord, show us the Father!* "Believest thou not that I am in the Father, and that the Father is in me?" (reverse order here, showing Jesus' indicated relation to the Father is that of equals—an array, not a heirarchy)

This sickness is not unto death, but for the glory of God, that the Son of God may be glorified by it.	11-4	If I say to you "taking that poison will not kill you, but give me a chance to heal you," I'd expect dubious glances at best as I cavalierly imply that I'm above all natural phenomena and can work miracles at will. And that is apparently how the disciples heard this claim, perhaps exchanging dubious glances among themselves. But Jesus' track record at this point was so well established that they saw it as another in a long string of unbelievables that came true in spite of obvious impossibility. And note the incredible boldness: Jesus asserts that the glory of God would be served and enhanced by what a man intended to do! A man may retrospectively say "I really honored God by doing ____," but to announce in advance that one's action will glorify God leaves no bridge unburned—either perform, or be scuttled by the God who *according to truth* will judge each by *thy own words*. Once mouthed, we must perform the thing uttered.
...he remained two days...	11-6	While I have only been cataloging verbal claims made by Jesus himself about himself, if actions were taken as non-verbal claims, the action of staying on two days insured that Lazarus would be thoroughly dead. No sleight of hand, no careful manipulation of circumstances or staging like a magician, but instead a clearing the playing field of ancillary props or dubious elements, so that after the fact even Jesus' detractors could not but believe he had indeed raised a dead man as he predicted in 5:25-28. Thus, a virtual claim that no special preparation was required by one who had announced a year prior that only "the voice of the Son of God" was needed to raise dead.

...he stumbles because the light is not in him.	11-10	Huh? *IN HIM??* One expects *he stumbles because the light of the sun is not visible at night.* But no, that is not what Jesus said, the manuscripts all agree with this reading, so these are his words. Taking this literally as usual with Jesus' unfamiliar pronouncements, one concludes that he is speaking of a reality of which modern science (with perhaps the exception of the emergent Bio-Photonics) is ignorant. I'll not go out on a limb to say how light *inside* one would enable walking when it's a dark night, but Jesus' track record of stating things obvious to an inhabitant of the heavens that we earthbound folks are missing, is too consistent to ignore. I see this as a claim to a knowledge about light that 21st century science does not possess.
Lazarus, our friend, has fallen asleep...	11-11	Stated as a fact, not a supposition, Jesus claims that he knows without being present when someone dies…
...but I go that I may awake him out of sleep.	11-11	...and strengthens the claim of an unusual acquaintance with death by saying he would override its power. He will raise a man dead and buried, on his fourth day in the grave. In this verse his motivation is that the disciples may believe. Earlier he had said it was (verse 4) for the glory of God. Later on it is obvious to all onlookers that love for Lazarus and his sisters played a part. Then he says in his prayer it is also for the crowd around, that they may believe. In verses 24-5 both his waiting and his subsequent raising was for Martha's faith. Following each of these threads we find perfect consistency leading to this event and lending strong circumstantial verification consistent with both these claims.
Jesus therefore then said to them plainly, Lazarus has died.	11-14	A repetition of the previous claim, stated baldly for the disciples' benefit.

Thy brother shall rise again.	11-23	That this was not a platitude "Well, don't feel bad, Lazarus will be part of the coming resurrection," but a claim, is evidenced from the continuing context. Jesus is testing whether she really believes what she has just said, by making a statement that can be taken either way. She defaults in her answer to platitudes she had acquired growing up Jewish, thus opening the way for for Jesus to restate the claim (below).
I am the resurrection and the life,	11-25	Men have claimed to be able to raise a single dead body, but never in the annals has a man claimed to *be* the resurrection, as well as *be* the life requisite to a dead body, once raised! Note that the "I am" here is in direct contrast with the Jewish notion of a general resurrection: Jesus in this claim inserts himself into the center of that mystery, at once disrupting the vague conception of what the coming resurrection would entail, and clarifying details that he had begun to sketch out in his earlier claims (see chapter 5:21 ff). If you—like Jonah, Noah, or Jesus—come preaching the wholesale destruction of an entire city or the entire race of mankind, the question of survivors arises. Jesus' claim here is that the gateway between the old Adam creation which is being destroyed and the new creation is resurrection life. Survivors enter through it. And he, Jesus, is the resurrection and the life, that gateway. One of the most powerful claims in this litany.
...he that believes on me, though he has died, shall live...	11-25	Take this as Martha perhaps did, as a reference to her brother Lazarus. Or take it in the absolute as most believers of Jesus have ever since, as a promise applicable to themselves. Demonstrated literally and immediately in Lazarus, millions of Christians since him claim it in another way as they approach literal death: they do so with the firm assurance that beyond it lies life with Christ.

...and he that lives and believes on me shall never die.	**11-26**	See comment above, and note that this claim introduces a new meaning for the word *death*. It's finality is gone. What was perceived as a bottomless pit since Cain introduced it becomes a *portal* — as several prophets had intimated. "Death, where is thy sting?" A claim when spoken by Jesus, a new species of encountering death as a victor rather than victim, by *martyrs,* a new kind of spectacle in the Roman world, calling for a new word to describe such: *Christians.*
Did I not say to thee, that if thou shouldest believe, thou shouldest see the glory of God?	**11-40**	This is a peculiarly Jewish claim: "glory of God" is not a household term in American households, nor among ancient pagan households, but one long connected with Moses, David, Solomon, Isaiah, Ezekiel, to name a few. The underlying commonality was physical and spiritual brightness, pureness, fearsomeness, transitoriness (for mortals witnessing) majesty, power and holy connectedness only with the divine. Moses longed for a glimpse of it, Jesus here offers to show it as curator to a less distinguished personage, a woman. Unused to casual reference to the things of Another, onlookers like Martha would expect all the above if privileged to see it. Thus Jesus' claims here go far beyond what all other mortals had dared speak of, or interact with. Note also Jesus' sharpness with Martha, witnessing to the attitude of one familiar with that glory.
Father, I thank thee...	**11-41**	Quite simply the first time in human history that a man publicly looked up and said "Father." More than a claim to familiarity, this was a first, enumerating from Adam onward. The Greek verb is in *vocative* case, reserved for direct address or colloquy.

...thou hast heard me, but I knew that thou always hearest me	**11-41**	How is this a claim? Protocol demands that before beginning to speak to a dignitary, you first secure an audience, access to their ear (or eye if writing), then obtain permission to address them using familiar words or a translator if demanded. In this case Jesus demonstrates by doing what he had taught the crowds concerning address to "your Father in heaven." He looks up, signalling that he wishes to speak, and receiving no signal that the constant, on-going colloquy he enjoyed with the Father was interrupted, *continues his (internal, unheard) dialog but now aloud* so as to show the crowds how an address to God may flow. Thus the implicit claim here is that he constantly enjoyed back and forth exchange with the God he had taught them to acknowledge by the new term, Father.
Lazarus, come forth!	**11-43**	This claim was verified in under a minute, so it is no longer a claim but an eye-witnessed ability to raise the dead.
The hour is come that the son of man should be glorified.	**12-23**	As noted several times already, another claim of Jesus to be independent of ordinary human time. Unlike most men, he consistently anticipated what was coming and thus was free to act rather than react in knee-jerk fashion.
...a grain of wheat remains but a solitary grain unless it first falls into the ground and dies. Yet if it die, it brings forth a rich harvest.	**12-24**	In comparing himself to a grain of wheat multiplying upon dying to its own existence, he was claiming that (see comment on 11:25 and earlier) a whole new race of men would result from his dying to flesh and blood life. The fact that he would leave his blood (with the life peculiar to that) in the earth, arise from the dead, and begin communicating that new life to men, was a claim of monstrous proportions. Doubtless Philip, Andrew and the other disciples had no understanding of this claim until after that life had been communicated to them by a risen Jesus.

...where I am, there, too, will my servant be.	**12-26**	this can be taken as a simple statement of fact: when you see a man, you are not surprised to see his servant nearby. But coming from a man invested with the power Jesus was claiming and demonstrating, his followers have expanded this statement into a claim. For them it includes the expectation that as his servants, if he rises from the dead, they will also; if he ascends to heaven, they will also. Thus this claim has acquired thousands if not millions of expectant hearers.
If any one serve me, him shall the Father honor.	**12-26**	Doesn't this grab your heartstrings? Here is someone who could have told you unbelievable details about where he was thirty-odd years ago—not bragging about that fact but telling you how *you* can be honored by God the Father. Here I repeat is someone who was in the bosom of God the Father a short time before and minutes away from a first for men—the honor of *getting an audible answer to prayer by a voice from heaven* in presence of witnesses...serving you. And apparently no one listened, far less took up his invitation to be honored by the Father. Again, a claim by Jesus that had never entered into a human mind.

Now is my soul troubled, and what shall I say? Father, save me from this hour(?) But on account of this have I come to this hour. Father glorify thy name.	12-28	Not a new claim but rather a demonstration of the truth of a previous claim, *I do always the things pleasing to Him.* (8:29) Unsought and uncrowned by his own people, here a second contingent of Gentiles seeks Jesus out to honor him. Rather than using their adulation to shame his own nation, he replies with an off-putting message delivered by Philip and Andrew. The eyes of the Father had watched four milennia for such Godlike action in a man on earth. Pleased as never before, the Father does an unprecedented thing: He replies to a man's request by a voice of words as though in a conversation, replying: *I both have glorified and will glorify [it] again!* And Jesus, faced with the pathos of rejection by Israel and the ethos of being singled out for unprecedented honor by God, responds as only a man on earth can, *now is my soul troubled.* But how is this a claim, you may ask. He could only be saying these words, acting this way, if he were setting out to demonstrate in actual human life that he is the second man, the last Adam. Every act he performed in small and in great, demonstrated the truth of this claim.
Not on my account has this voice come, but on yours.	12-30	Picture the scene. Jesus is in conversation with Philip and Andrew, telling them how to respond to the Greeks seeking him. He considers, gives an elliptical answer, feels troubled and begins to say so in the immediate hearing of all present. But his Father touches the mute button and makes audible to Andrew, Philip, the crowd and probably also the Greeks, the continuous ongoing conversation between Himself and Jesus. Jesus is the only one not surprised, since the flow of dialog is uninterrupted for him. Hearers speculate whether merely thunder or perhaps an angelic voice is the source of the unexpected sound. Jesus settles the question. Not only does he tell them what the sound was, but (a second claim) why it came.

Now is the judgment (Gr. Krisis) of this world...	12-31	Less than three years prior, Jesus had intimated to a leading Pharisee that the crisis announced by their prophets was imminent. (see his discourse to Nicodemus in chapter 3). Here, Jesus adds cosmic events to the previously noticed (2:4) claim of personally observing an invisible clock and calendar. He announces a (literally) earth-shaking event in this claim: the close of the period begun in the garden of Eden and terminating upon his "lifting up."
...now shall the prince (archon) of this world be cast out.	12-31	When a General announces intent to clear out the enemy by an assault, his words are noted and he is held to his claim. Here Jesus predicts the time and occasion of the defeat and dethronement of mankind's enemy, a being who held sway ever since our parents took of the tree and ate. These words are doubtless directed equally at both spiritual as well as human listeners; at this point such had already witnessed the successful birth from a virgin womb, the impeccable untarnished humanity resident in Jesus, his dismissal of Satan's attempt to make him fall like Adam—and now Jesus' throwing down the gauntlet, reminiscent of the challenge to Goliath: *Who is this uncircumcised Philistine, that he should defy the ranks of the living God...I will smite thee and take thy head from thee.*
...and I, if I be lifted up out of the earth, will draw all {men} to me.	12-32	John the author comments that in these words Jesus was signifying by what death he would die. To signify is to put into a visible symbol what is otherwise expressed solely in audible or written words. Thus the esoteric becomes exoteric—words understood by scholarly scribes and Pharisees become plain to common folk as they do here. Even unlettered people knew "lifting up" could mean *exalt* as Pharoah's butler, or *decapitate* as his poor baker. So when they saw Jesus lifted up on a cross, darkness at noon, an earthquake at his death, wordless signs spoke to them louder than plainly spoken words to instructed masters. The crowds *having seen the things that took place returned,* Luke tells us, *beating their breasts.*

Yet a little while is the light amongst you.	12-35	Again, Jesus is here claiming to be the light of the world, a claim easy to challenge if made by any living man in my acquaintance.
But Jesus cried and said, He that believes on (Gr. eis) me, believes not on me but on him that sent me; and he that beholds me, beholds him that sent me...	12-44	A many faceted claim. First, that his words and his works were so demonstrably intertwined as to support each other without flaw or exception. He had claimed (8:25) to *be* what his words proclaimed: thus setting himself up as perfect and making his words and actions the object of intense scrutiny. Second, that he was such a mirror-perfect image of the One he was representing as heaven's ambassador that a mere glance at any of his words or doings was exchangeable for a glance at their Diety. It was obvious that he was sent—like Abraham's servant he sought only the interests of his master, never straying from that bent to aggrandize or enrich himself. And thus upon this claim being fulfilled, his ambassadorial mission was ended. Like Noah, Jeremiah or Jonah, he had declared the end of God's patience with the world that then was, the nation of Israel, the city of Ninevah. But unlike them, Jesus had now made guilty the entire world: those who could and did know of God the Father Himself, had seen him and rejected his acknowledged son. And so the gospel account of Jesus' mission, his ambassadorial charge, closes with this final discourse that Jesus "cried"—an afterword I believe, out of chronological sequence but consonant with the last action recorded "he went away and hid himself from them," i.e., hid himself having made a last, final outcry.
...he that beholds me, beholds him that sent me. (2nd quote)	12-44	(revisit the above claim to observe a less obvious claim). Prophets all give signs (with the exception of John the baptiser). Jesus gave signs. But here he goes beyond mere signs that *point*, to an image that *is*. Beholders of Jesus had the immediacy of all their senses experiencing the Father, rather than mediated, inductively or deductively-reasoned evidence of the Father. Thus this claim goes beyond all the prophets, who pointed at signs...Jesus points to himself.

I am come into the world [as] light...	12-46	Jesus had before claimed to be the light of the world (3:22, 8:12 ff, 9:5, 12:35), offering his person as *objet de la foi*, an object of faith as the raised serpent of Moses. Onlookers received in a glance what was otherwise unavailable to them. This is in stark contrast to what Jesus claims a few sentences later, that his mission was not to judge the world: he came as light, not as judge. Note the many subject closures in this final section, chapter 12. An example is v.37 where *they believed not on him* closes what began in 1:11 *his own received him not*. Chapters one thru twelve being the record of representative incidents, claims, sayings, facts, beseechings by the ambassador. They contain precisely seven signs, as promised in 2:11 and 4:54. We come to closure of that mission here in chapter twelve. Moses had given ten signs, Jesus seven. An eighth will be added in what is really John's appendix (chapter 21) but the ambassador's mission proper closes with these signs rejected. His claim of coming as light is the ambassador's farewell to the people and leaders of Israel, as his formal farewell to his disciples is chapters 13 thru 16, and his farewell from the foreign country before returning to the Father occupies all of chapter 17.
I judge him not, for I am not come that I might judge the world, but that I might save the world.	12-47	Lest they misunderstand, Jesus again repeats the claim that his mission was not to act in the capacity of judge, but that of savior. Rejected personally, his words would judge erstwhile hearers in the last day, as the next claim below declares.

He that rejects me and does not receive my words, has him who judges him: the word which I have spoken, that shall judge him in the last day.	**12-48**	Can you imagine being accosted by such words today, by anyone in the sphere of your acquaintance? Even here in NYC where I *can* almost imagine it, folks would just quietly turn their heads away as they do from someone using captive attention of a subway car to throw megalomaniac words in your face. But that is not what we have here: Jesus' every word and action to that point secured him a credible audience that silently—perhaps with side-wise glances—nonetheless considered such words. Among the common people as well as the leadership, he simply could not be dismissed. The fact that they were spoken, have stood for 2000 years, and continue to get identical response from each successive generation, demonstrates their universal applicability over two millennia. No better, or more individual-touching criteria could be devised whereby to gauge humankind's response. I say this to anticipate the question *how can one man's words to a few folks in a small mid-eastern country twenty centuries ago serve to put the entire race of men on trial?* I'll turn that around: How would you do it if you were God, mankind's maker?
For I have not spoken from myself...	**12-49**	Note that this expression is used of Son and Spirit, never of the Father. Thus Jesus is claiming here that to attribute these sayings to him as proceeding merely from himself is a terrible blunder: an ambassador's words are those of a plenipotentiary empowered by another, by a Father of whom they said *he is our God.*(8:54). Rejecting the messenger and his words, they rejected his Sender; Rejecting him in whom all the promises of God are vested, they cut themselves off from the very promises they sought!

...but the Father who sent me has himself given me commandment what I should 1) say (eipon) and 2) what I should speak (lalein)...	12-49 (2)	A double claim, noting that Jesus distinguishes between the subject matter and the actual words employed in which to offer it. If I said "uncle Arthur not only asked me to talk to you about this, but insisted I not misrepresent it by using the wrong words," you would pay particular attention to both my expressions as well as to the general subject. So here, and the reason for two Greek words rather than one.
...and I know that his commandment is life eternal	12-50	Lest we think "eternal life" simply means unending existence (whether in blood and flesh or else how) Jesus here equates the Father's commandment with eternal life, as he will equate knowing the Father with eternal life in chapter 17. This claim of Jesus is completely consistent with the many others we've catalogued in which he speaks of the Father, of His feelings and His surroundings just as you or I speak of our own fathers. And note again, this claim continues to make good the claim (3:12) to a leader in Israel that he would like to speak of heavenly, unknown things rather than limit himself to repeating sayings of their prophets — all of which concerned the earth. Apparently no one had the temerity to ask him to speak of heavenly things—even the disciples fail to ask questions like *what were you doing forty years ago? Did you have a body then? Is heaven a place or a condition? Do angels all have wings? How often does Satan present himself before God?* and so on...

What therefore I speak, as the Father has said to me, so I speak.	12-50	Whether this "cry" of Jesus was spoken at that occasion or is part of John's editorial summary in verses 37 to 50, i.e., a repeated refrain of Jesus made on an unspecified or on more than one occasion, is not clear. The claims listed above however, stand in either case. At a funeral or other commemoration of an individual's accomplishments, statements like these are often made by ourselves, not so much recalling a particular conversation or speech, but a characteristic theme on the mind and lips of the one quoted. And note again that the word *as* in this verse sets aside the modern phenomenon of 'channeled' speech, in which a person's tongue and larynx are yielded to a spirit other than the spirit of the man himself. Jesus had the liberty to phrase or rephrase what he heard from the Father as he wished. He was not (as Edgar Cayce etc) yielding his recumbent body to another being who spoke using the speech organs of the submissive human.
["knowing his hour had come," "that he should depart out of this world to the Father" "loved them to the end (or completely)," "knowing that the Father had given all things into his hands," "and that he came out from God," "and was going to God,"]	13-1 to 3 (6)	I bracket these six claims since they are made of Jesus by John the writer, rather than spoken by Jesus. Note that in these "upper room" discourses from 13 thru 16, John adds such explanatory statements with greater frequency than elsewhere — statements that would be claims if said by Jesus verbally as all the other claims listed so far.
Ye call me the Teacher and the Lord, and ye say well, for I am.	13-13	Note that by accepting the two designations THE Teacher and THE Lord rather than "ye call me teacher and lord," Jesus is claiming to be more than a rabbi among rabbis.

I tell you now, before it happens	13-19	Not only would what the scriptures had said happen, but the manner and time and place of the happening was choreographed rather than merely known by Jesus, as we'll see shortly. Thus, this is a claim by Jesus that he could both predict and control in advance, happenings in this world. Imagine Caesar saying this about Brutus and his gang who plotted to kill him; he would assuredly have acted *so as to prevent his assassination*, acting out of fear that his life was about to be snuffed out. Not so Jesus!
I tell you...that I am the one who truly *is*.	13-19	Jesus repeats privately to his disciples what he had three times claimed before Israel's leaders: to *be* existence rather than to *derive* existence from a greater source. (see 7:28, 8:24, 8:28)
...him who has sent me.	13-20	Again, the oft-repeated claim to have been sent from elsewhere to the earth by one he knew as Father, they as Adonai.
...one of you shall deliver me up.	13-21	He knew both *that* and *who* would deliver him up, in this claim. Spoken of necessity, plainly and clearly rather than accusingly or petulantly as others in like circumstances might do. Anyone aware of such a solemn, unanticipated happening would surely wish to share the awareness. Elisha is thusly approached by the sons of the prophets "do you know that Jehovah will take away your master from over your head today?" and answers "I also know it: be silent!" It cannot be that the disciples should proceed unwarned that one will arise from among their own group to deliver Jesus up. Jesus does not offer this as a feeling or opinion so as to be proved right or demonstrate his foreknowledge, but "I tell you now, before it happens that when it happens you may believe that I am the one who truly *is.*" Jesus' claims are never empty or spoken to simply attract attention.

Now is the son of man glorified, and God is glorified in him.	13-31	If I say to you "I just did a big favor for the president that he will thank me for" you might pause to see if I am pulling your leg. But Jesus had announced early on (8:28) that he did nothing "of himself," ever acting solely for the Father's glory, and "now," was an instance. The same deliberateness with which he made the initial claim is in evidence here — not shouted as a "Eureka!" moment but simply laid out for their observation...incidentally fulfilling Isaiah's prophecy that the coming one would not "cry, nor lift up his voice nor cause it to be heard in the street." The calm dignity that accompanied all Jesus' claims sets them apart, lending them an unequalled credibility. The added claim that God would glorify him awaited fulfilment: his resurrection as the first man ever raised up from among the Adamic dead, never to die again, seems to be what Jesus is announcing.

If God be glorified in him, God also shall glorify him in himself, and shall glorify him immediately.	13-32	Having made such an unusual (for a Jewish prophet) claim, Jesus now adds to and strengthens it...well aware that his every word was watched, noted, and marvelled at even while not being understood as here by his disciples. While an empty boaster if making such claims would not expect to be taken seriously, Jesus continues on, knowing that understanding could only come later as the disciples watched that glorification take place, and felt the Spirit dwelling within them open their understanding. Note the word *immediately*...only one utterly confident that he spoke well-known truth would dare add such a detail. There is no hint of timorousness in Jesus' many claims involving intimacy with Deity. Again, I am reminded of <u>The Prince and the Pauper</u> where a supposed street lad suddenly and consistently speaks the King's English with the careless abandon of one brought up in it. Jesus' words are not the cautious, coached words of an imitator but the natural, flowing utterances of one come from the heavens as he claimed. False prophets in Israel gave themselves away by needless repetition and careful collusion (see, for example Jer 27 to 29 or 1 Kings 22) and if a God-fearing prophet even thought about uttering such words, he would hesitate from fear of being struck down like Uzzah. Not so Jesus: the ring of truth was ever in his words: integrity is the companion of truth.
...as I said to the Jews, Where I go ye cannot come, I say to you also now.	13-33	When someone makes a claim like this, you take it as a challenge...*ye cannot come!* The disciples, while a bit put-off, were by now accustomed to Jesus' frequent unusual sayings and challenges to their leaders. A claim like this is not quickly forgotten, and doubtless was clearly understood after they saw what he was speaking of when he said "I go to prepare," or "I will not leave you orphans," and so on in this prolonged discourse that night.

By this shall all know that ye are disciples of mine, if ye have love amongst yourselves.	**13-35**	A claim amply proved over time, beginning with Tertullian, who remarks that pagans often make the comment 'See how these Christians love one another'. The popularization of love in current Western and even more recently Eastern culture, takes as a given that we have come into fascination with love as the prime mover by simple life experience. This, while true from an existential standpoint, fails to credit the man prior to whom love was seldom employed as he, Jesus, introduced it. Is there any example in pagan writ of Love being a major attribute of deity, love, that is, as an essential of deity's being, rather than lust between demi-gods? I know of none.
The cock shall not crow till thou hast denied me thrice.	**13-38**	What is interesting about this claim is the ordinaryness with which it was spoken—conversational repartee. By this time, three years into following Jesus, the disciples had learned not to discount Jesus' sayings, difficult as that often was. The stark contrast of Jesus' prevision of imminent events and Peter's plaintive words draws out "*thy life* thou wilt lay down for me?." Peter, having discounted Jesus' entré, "thou canst not follow me now," and not willing to risk discounting these latter words, lapses into silence, a silence punctuated a few hours later by three increasingly vitriolic outbursts suddenly broken by another sound—a cock crowing. At that, two men turn toward each other across the palace hall, their eyes meet—eloquent acknowledgment of a simply spoken claim.

....ye believe on God...believe also on me!	14:1	You can't believe "on" (Greek *eis*) a person unless in some way they exceed what your senses can take in. John uses this expression many times beginning in 3:15 where we noted Jesus thereby claimed he was not an ordinary mortal whom it would be superstition to believe on. You can and do believe men when they speak; believing *on* another mortal is either an act of superstition or a confession that you own that mortal as immeasurably greater than yourself. The latter is obviously Jesus' meaning here as he expands their existing belief on God to include the man standing before them, an incredibly difficult thing to do because of that very humanity, and indeed, the charge for which the leadership crucified him.
In my Father's house are many abodes...	14:2	A claim that Adonai, now called Father by Jesus, has a "house," a mansion (see KJV) of many rooms awaiting guests! Suppose two boys are playing, get hungry, and the one says "Let's go to my daddy's house, mommie is making brownies and ice cream today." Jesus, laden with knowledge of heavenly things but never queried about them, again begins in earnest on this last night on earth to open up the heavens he knew so well. It's as though on the way to the brownies, one boy remembers, halts and says "oh, I forgot! you can't come as you are to my daddy's house." Previous attempts by Jesus to inform the temple guardians that they were really servants in his Father's house had gone unheeded. His attempt to get Nicodemus to understand that getting into the earthly kingdom of their messiah required getting born all over again went misunderstood among Israel's leadership—heavenly things were not looked for. Small wonder that when a woman at Jacob's well *did* ask after heavenly things, she received and went away with more than brownies and ice cream! She got what the disciples could have gotten and didn't: "poor (in spirit) have good news proclaimed to them."

I go to prepare you a place	14-2	While a casual hearer would hardly see this as a claim, Jesus is speaking here to both casual hearers—unschooled disciples—and to future proclaimers of his yet to be accomplished actions. To a cognoscenti trained in the long tradition of the rabbis, such words are radical heresy: How could an all-knowing God whose purposes determine what is, have been caught blind-sided so as to necessitate someone preparing a place He had not foreseen and prepared for? It would appear that Jesus' desire to have with him where he *is* (chap 17:24) the spoils of victory—his twelve and all who believed thru their word—was unforeseen by the heavens until that moment. The twelve expected to continue with him, totally unaware that the cross lay ahead, and because of that expectation Jesus adds "if it were not so I would have told you." In other words, *not only will I send an interim comforter, but I will ensure that among the many abodes of my Father place will be found for you.*
I am coming again...	14-3	General MacArthur's famous words when leaving the Philippines were *I shall return*. Three quarters of a century later they are still recalled, a stirring example of a public claim, and one which frequently caused MacArthur pain as he waited and saw his troops decimated by enemy forces. Two thousand years later Jesus is still waiting, his troops joining in his "hour of patience," Can you imagine someone trying to spiritualize MacArthur's words to make them say he meant he'd be with them in spirit, or by dwelling in their memories?

...and shall receive you unto myself that where I am ye also may be.	14-3	Note the utter confidence with which this claim was spoken. In his prayer to the Father a few hours later Jesus asks specifically for this: *Father, as to those thou hast given me, I desire that where I am they also may be with me;"* here he asserts the consequences of that asking will come true. While the day and hour of that coming is entirely the province of the Father to decide (Acts 1:7), the fact of it, once asked for, is as good as the reality itself. He had taught them to ask expecting; here he shows them how. Compare this with the above and ask whether MacArthur could have gone the extra length in his claim.
And ye know where I go, and ye know the way.	14-4	A teacher imparts confidence to instill his teaching in the students, sometimes crediting them with what they are doubtful they have. So here, Jesus claims (and proves) that they did know that he would be returning to where he came from, vaguely familiar as that place/condition seemed at that moment to his disciples. Thus Jesus' rejoinder *I AM the way, and the truth, and the life* to Thomas' *we know NOT* was to insert the simple but radically new fact that knowing Jesus makes the acquisition of facts obsolete! Adam's act not only had distanced mankind from God, but had made the acquisition of knowledge into a tedious, plodding thing fraught with cares, mistakes, a never ending process. The end of this condition for mankind is preannounced by Jesus in the above words, putting *himself* where the disciples expected to garner and store fragments of knowledge. John will expand this in his epistle to tell his fellow disciples *ye know all things and have no need that anyone should teach you...abide in HIM* (not in facts, but in the person of Jesus). So in this claim Jesus tells them what they already knew—less a claim than a whole new way of knowing, now shared by all Jesus' own.

I am the way, and the truth, and the life...	14-6 (3)	Often quoted, these are three separate claims as the *ands* that couple them (missing in the KJV) indicate. Even if Jesus' meaning is less than clear there is no mistaking the magnitude of these three claims. Founders of the world's religions may assert their teaching to be truth, or a way to the truth, but Jesus leaves no doubt that he is the only way to the Father, scuttling all others from the place he claims for himself alone. If Jesus is not who he says he is, claims like this would become simple arrogance, easily detected.
...no one comes to the Father unless by me.	14-6	This claim to be the only way to the Father makes Jesus' enemies to squirm, cavil, or despise—what sort of humility asserts itself as the exclusive way to God? Christians on the other hand, overextend this claim beyond Jesus' obvious meaning to say that *God* is now unapproachable save thru Jesus, but Jesus says "the *Father*," clearly distinguished from "God" (as well as coidentified at times) by John. God still is approached as He ever has been by the children of men; not so the Father, Who can only be approached thru Jesus.
...ye know him and have seen him.	14-7	As noted above, this is less a claim of Jesus than a teaching device to impart confidence and thereby accelerate learning—something any disciple of Jesus will heartily agree they need in order to understand Jesus' words! Paul characterizes God as one who "calls the things that be not as being" — a striking claim in this context. We can't speak something into existence by calling. God can. So Jesus here tells his disciples they knew the Father and had seen Him...in answer to Phillip's assertion that none of them had any clue to knowing the Father or having seen Him. Did the teaching device work? Yes, but we'll have to wait until chapter 16:29-30 to see how.

He that has seen me has seen the Father	14-9	We are unaccustomed to ordinary people making extravagent, unembellished claims like this in ordinary conversation. I'm sure the disciples were no exception, in fact, the response shows exasperation rather than acceptance as Philip speaks for the group, *Lord show us the Father and it suffices us*. Extravagant? yes. Believable? with difficulty. Common? yes. Jesus made so many claims like this in such an unaffected and ordinary manner that, but for his body language backing them up, folks would have immediately backed away from the words alone. The claim here is that he is better than a mirror image of the Father, since a mirror can be obscured, drop out of range, be rotely reflective-only...unlike Jesus who (see 8:28 above) instead of channeling words, spoke them from his own personal center with understanding and emphasis and passion, something I believe unparalled then or now.
The words which I speak to you I do not speak from myself; but the Father who abides in me, he does his works.	14-10 (3)	If an ambassador is challenged in speaking by "what you are saying is unbelievable!" he can pause, he can stop, he can get upset, he can shout back, he can produce his letter of mission, he can rephrase his words, he can demonstrate, he can warn or threaten, he can quietly repeat with well-chosen emphasis, he can gesticulate pounding his fist or he can get his sender on the phone—an almost endless number of options. Protocol guides him in his choice of which to pick. So here. Jesus can choose whether to act as a teacher, a friend, a heavenly messenger charged with getting his message across, a lover of mankind, the revealer of the Father, a shepherd of another's sheep, a washer of disciples' feet, to name a few. This gives him a wide range of posture(s) to speak from, and he chooses to repeat the claim in language he has used before. Note we are looking at three distinct claims here: 1) his words are sourced in the Father, 2) the Father abides in him, and 3) the Father does his [own] works—an expression capable of more than one interpretation.

I am in the Father, and the Father in me	**14-11**	When someone says something new and less than crystal clear to you, you back off and wait for what he says next, upon noting your puzzled expression. If instead of explaining he avers the same thing in stronger language, you note that he has chosen to address your puzzlement by emphasis rather than a long explanation. If you regard the speaker as a teacher more knowledgeable than yourself, you may concede in silence, tucking away the words and hoping they will get plain as he goes on or as your understanding grows. Jesus' claim here to be "in the Father" and "the Father [is] in me" were certainly new concepts to the disciples and, delivered as an explanation that should be obvious in meaning to them ...well, I'm afraid my reaction of silence would have been just as loud as theirs. Happily we'll find, as I keep hinting, that after several hours of this, resolution does indeed arrive at the end of the long night (chap 16).

He that believes on me, the works which I do shall he do also, and he shall do greater than these, because I go to the Father.	14-12	When you speak in private to close associates, your words and claims fall on ears that expect privileged communications. The eleven disciples sequestered in an upper room found at least perplexing if not unbelieveable, most of Jesus' words that last night. Imagine sitting across from Mozart as he relates that upon his leaving you the next day, you will be empowered to write better musical pieces than he. Jesus says this and, equally puzzling, the reason why. "I go to the Father" conveyed nothing familiar or comprehensible to them, and thus mere words devoid of definite meaning. Repeated enigmatic utterances like this characterized the entire night, but for the brief action of washing their feet—a stark contrast to Jesus' mystical words! But while thinking of great men with great claims, whether Jesus or Mozart or Nebuchadnezzar— which of them do you think would without a word wash your feet to demonstrate the reality of their words? Taking it a little farther, how many authors prior to the gospel writers ever depicted such an action in their Odysseys, Eddas, Buddhacarita, Avesta, or Vedas?
...whatsoever ye shall ask in my name, this will I do, that the Father may be glorified in the son.	14-13	This claim builds on the previous: Absent, he would yet hear and answer their requests from the place he would be, invisible to them. Also implicit is the claim that so doing would not only be observed by God himself, but would glorify God the Father! The claim presumes an understanding of these very mystical happenings by proposing the metaphor (or reality) of a father/son relationship existing in the place where he would be after returning from the earth to the Father, presumably heaven.

If ye shall ask anything in my name, I will do it.	14-14	In this repetition of the previous claim Jesus strengthens and removes possible ambiguity by asserting that the son he was speaking of is indeed himself—a divine person if son to God the Father. From the casualness with which he makes such a monstrous claim over and over, it is apparent to any listener that he believes it himself. Men falsely claiming such a position, title and birthright always give a hint that they know deep down the claim is not valid. The fact that Jesus' constant claims, his comments based on them, projections assuming them etc etc are consistent provides another evidence of believability to any common listener. I would say *proof* but that word has fallen into bad company in today's Western science-dominated world. The second part of this claim is tested. For two thousand years men have asked of Jesus and received—Jesus' *anything* means just that. No need to limit or qualify the things asked for—Jesus' other claims assert all things in heaven and earth are his, as are all that the Father Himself has. Kings may say *ask up to the half of my kingdom* as Herod, but Jesus' failure to limit or qualify is totally consistent with his personality, his other words, his accessibility to men and his non-concern with material possessions.
And I will beg the Father...	14-16	Why is this simple statement a claim? Because it uses the familiar form of *ask* rather than the formal. Greek, as many other languages has words that are only used in situations where intimacy or equality exists, and other words for use by an inferior when addressing a superior. Thus Jesus here is claiming to be on equal, intimate footing with God the Father Himself, rather than a supplicant carefully addressing the Father according to protocol. (the Greek words are *erotao* and *aiteo)*.

1)...and He will give you 2) another Comforter, 3) that he may be with you forever 4) the Spirit of truth, 5) whom the world cannot receive, 6) because it does not see him nor know him; 7) but ye know him, 8) for he abides with you, 9) and shall be in you.	**14-16** (9)	This is too much! Every statement in these two sentences is a claim, or an assertion of knowledge about things totally foreign and unknown to his hearers. *He will give you* presumes Jesus knows God well enough to speak for him, a strong claim. *Another Comforter* introduces something/someone neither disciples, scribes or the world had ever heard of. *That He may be with you forever* confidently asserts a furthur detail about that comforter. *The Spirit of Truth,* Jesus claims, is another name by which the Comforter is known—again a new claim of familiarity with Godhead that no emissary or ambassador would venture to make on his own. *Ye know Him* tells the disciples plainly something they would absolutely have denied if asked, thereby Jesus is claiming to know their state of knowledge better than the disciples themselves! By saying *Whom the world cannot receive,* Jesus is asserting a definite fact about something/someone up to then only known vaguely as associated with the power of God. *It [the world] does not see him or know Him* is a predictive claim regarding how the world would react to the Spirit of Truth. *But ye know Him* again asserts the disciples had a knowledge they were personally unaware of. *He abides with you* and *shall be in you* are assertive claims not of knowledge merely, but of experimentally verifiable facts, present and future. This "loaded" language so characterizes Jesus' speech as to render it gibberish to the uninitiated—exactly what many NT scholars declare it to be. [i.e.,"replete with repetitive and nearly interminable speeches p.261; inflated rhetoric p.270; dignified but boring speeches that sometimes run to several pages p.271; airless solemnity that leaves us begging p.271 in <u>Desire of the Everlasting Hills</u> by Thomas Cahill] Those with ears to hear readily acquire new forms of expression, an esoteric language by which disciples now recognize one another.

I will not leave you orphans; I am coming to you.	**14-18**	Spoken in the context of going away, of "coming" again, of his absence creating a void, this claim suggests Jesus knew how they would soon feel upon his crucifixion and burial—orphaned children—and how he would remedy that terrible feeling. If you were to have asked these disciples eight weeks later if what he said had come true, ("do you still feel like orphans?") you would have gotten a resounding No! In fact, listen to Peter as he addresses his assembled nation: "Jesus the Nazaraean...ye have slain... God has raised up...he [unlike David] has not been left in Hades...[but] God raised up... exalted...given him the promised Spirit...made him both Lord and Christ." Acts 2. It is no less paradoxical than true to fact that unlike other men, the farther away you get from Jesus' brief life the better you understand him, as Peter did two months later. This is why academic search for the "historical Jesus" is so fruitless and silly. Academics do not understand the above claims, on the contrary most see them as gibberish. To such Jesus' words are well addressed: "If I have spoken earthly things to you and you do not understand, how if I say the heavenly things to you will you understand?" Claims posited on previous claims demand understanding from the ground up. Simple fishermen like Peter learned that, as the earthly Jesus dimmed and the real Jesus continued speaking to orphaned disciples from the place to which he had gone. Academics will find little source material in the three years of Jesus' indentured servitude. A true and exemplary servant, he never spoke of himself, leaving us without details that would "explain" who he was as a man and thus, why he acted as he did.

I am coming to you.	**14:18**	If you have been following Jesus' dialogue you will realize he is not speaking of his "second coming" here as he does in Matt 24 and 25. This claim is something never prophesied, encountered, or thought of before. That Holy Spirit by which Jesus had performed every action, every word while with them would come in the role of Comforter of his own, and so thoroughly take up residence in the bodies of Jesus' disciples that they would feel Jesus' feelings, understand his parables, empathize with his patience and impatience, groan with his groanings, do greater works than he! Fifty-odd days later Jesus came to them as he here announces. While bodily in the heavens, Jesus' spirit indwelling disciples was so real, so powerful as to transcend Jesus' bodily presence with them. That is how this claim was fulfilled — ask any believer! Jesus' claim *I am coming to you* — by sending his spirit when ascended — was an intimate, untried act in the Adam creation, but a formative all-affecting reality in the new man being formed upon Jesus' resurrection. To actually transfer one's spirit to another person is an act of intimacy that transcends the fondest wish of lovers, desires of every acolyte, apprentice of every master (think of Elisha and Elijah!), servants of a great kind lord and — admirers of the man Jesus. Paul expresses it this way: "We have received, not the spirit which is of the world, but the spirit which is of God." 1 Cor 2:12. Jesus is here; not bodily, but by his spirit.

Yet a little and the world sees me no longer; but ye see me;	**14-19**	The simplicity with which these words were spoken belies their awesome force, and the disciples while attempting to comprehend find them so outre as to challenge their ability to believe. They could indeed imagine Jesus being no longer with them—that point at least was seen after Jesus' many repetitions — but that they would somehow *not* be cut off from experiencing his presence once again turns a statement into an exotic claim. The conditions of daily life must be changed for this claim to come true, as Judas will protest in a moment.
...because I live ye also shall live.	**14-19**	Jesus never wearies of adding conundrum to riddle; of fresh building on premises not yet comprehended; of speaking in language reserved for magicians: e.g. *I'll be invisible to the world, but visible to you!*, of drawing conclusions from syllogisms lacking major or minor premises. As to his claim here "because I live you also shall live" — is he speaking of the life they currently possessed, of life in the new conditions alluded to, of life after death, or what? His speech serenely plows where never plow broke ground lending a certain *eclat* to these claims, inviting listeners to listen to the flow of words rather than granular details...what scripture calls *the power of the sound*. Again, Jesus speaks as one who believed his own statement that the coming comforter would bring to their remembrance all things he was speaking to them. This excused him from the need to explain what could not possibly make sense at this point. They could and did remember his strange words after the promised "comforter" arrived, supplying the enlightenment they craved to Jesus' obtuse words.

In that day ye shall know that I am in my Father and ye in me and I in you.	14-20	A claim requiring elucidation from the 'Spirit of Truth' Jesus spoke of earlier. The disciples were barely getting comfortable with this new name for God, 'Father', so when Jesus builds on that tremulous understanding by describing how he is "in" that Father and they were "in me" and Jesus "in you" ... he seems to be hanging upper structure on a shaky or non-existing lower structure. Nevertheless, it needed to be said, just as seeds with no resemblance to their flower need to be blindly placed in dark earth to germinate. Seed sowers know this. Word-sowers less often know it. Jesus knows it intimately and does it deftly. Germination time for these words was precisely fifty days, then they flowered.
...he that loves me shall be loved by my Father...	14-21	Once again, Jesus' willingness to commit the Father to an action (loving Jesus' disciples) is a claim to be on intimate terms with Deity, and of course by saying *my* Father, a claim to deity by Jesus himself.
...and I will love him and manifest himself to him.	14-21	Implied claim that he would be alive after being crucified, continue loving them, and be able as well to manifest himself to them in some unexplained condition, without (see 14:19) the world being directly aware of that manifesting.
...my Father will love him, and we will come to him...	14-23	Once again, a claim of intimacy with God the Father such that he can predict what God will feel! Then, by casually adding *we will come* he is delivering a claim, a promise he and his newly-introduced Father would be held to by these simple fishermen, as well as by the God who holds every man to the words that proceed from their mouth. And note in this context that Jesus' enemies too (just like Job's adversary) take note of spoken words to use against their speaker.

...and make our abode with him.	14-23	If the president shows up at your door with full entourage and says "We've come to call on you," you would feel honored to welcome him and the first lady. But if he signals his assistant to bring in luggage and says "we really would like to stay with you," you would find it unbelievable. Consider. Jesus has just claimed to be deity, claimed to be able to speak for God Himself, his Father, and now lays on you that the two of them want to stay with you. I can't imagine an iota of comprehension on the part of the disciples as he said it, forcing them to just store the words away hastily while hunkering down overwhelmed by a continuing onslaught of heavenly realities. Credible too-good-to-be-true words can be believed if you know and trust the speaker. Incredible too-good-to-be-true words create a whole different reaction in you.
...the word which ye hear is not mine but of the Father who has sent me.	14-24	Listening to the words of someone you've come to love and respect, one day you find that the words you've been enjoying are not his own but those of another person trying to reach you thru him! You would wonder who that other is and why he has chosen to reach you in this odd way. Actually Jesus told them from the beginning but they had doubtless filed his words away without understanding who the Father was, far less that He could be personally interested in them. When he told the Jews (8-26, 12-49) that the words he was speaking to them originated in the Father, their scornful response had been "show us this father of yours." But Jesus was charged with getting that across to a representative cadre of men, and up to this 'all-nighter' without visible success. Proof of his mission's success hinged on this, as we'll see when it happened (16:39) as well as in the ambassador's debriefing (chapter 17, especially verse 8)

...the Comforter, the Holy Spirit, whom the Father will send in my name...	14-26	By now it is clear (in retrospect, as we read these words!) that Jesus is arming them, outfitting them, sowing seeds of heavenly plants in the earthy ground of their hearts and minds, seeds that would shortly spring to life from darkened soil to produce a verdant growth beyond the world in patriachal times or Solomonic flourishing had never dreamed of! He continues speaking for the Father, confidently telling them exactly what this Person of the Deity would do in concert with the other Persons, a strong claim for a man to make of his God. (Note also, speaking again of sending, it is never the Father who is sent while both the Spirit and the Son are sent.)
...he shall teach you all things...	14-26	The new rulers of the world (Jesus' chosen ones) are told how and what they will learn upon his absence—how to retake the world in Jesus' name, learning daily from the Comforter's teaching. Peter experienced this on Simon the tanner's rooftop as, hungry, the Spirit not only reminded him of his Jewish upbringing but of Jesus' cleansing that went far beyond that prescribed in Leviticus or in the prophets saying *I will sprinkle clean water upon you [Israel] and ye [Israel] shall be clean* included Gentiles as well as Israel! Peter needed this teaching and Jesus' claim here was daily fulfilled in the disciples as well as in those that believed *through their word.* (chap 17:20)

...and will bring to your remembrance all the things which I have said to you.	14-26	Not only does Jesus undertake to speak for the Father as above without fear of correction, but now speaks for the Holy Spirit with the same confident poise. By contrast, listen to Paul: *as to the brother Apollos, I begged him much that he would go to you with the brethren, but it was not at all his will to go now...*Paul does not undertake to speak for a brother, even one he was quite close to. So not only is Jesus making a claim here that would come to pass, but is introducing the disciples to a whole new manner of relating to one another, i.e., do as we (the Persons of the Godhead) do; as he showed them earlier that evening washing feet. Such teaching, done without awareness of the learners, is more than the making of a claim. It fulfills the claim made earlier to Nicodemus that he had come with heavenly things to convey. (Side comment: If you have ever wondered, as I have, how John managed years later to recall granular detail of Jesus' mystical, seemingly unconnected statements like those in this section (Chapters 13-17), just credence Jesus' claim here that John would have help writing his gospel: *he will bring to your remembrance.* The Holy Spirit daily uses natural faculties like human memory to bring again what was thought to be lost.)
...I go to the Father...	14-28	While other men would have said *I am about to die in a few days,* Jesus speaks of his death as simply a step in his return to the Father, mission accomplished — rather than life violently wrested from him. He is thus claiming that his ambassadorial mission accomplished, he will be received back by his sender. Claims like this serve to acquaint us with how Jesus thought.

...my Father is greater than I.	14-28	Not a statement of modesty or false humility: aside from this claim and a few other like it, we would be utterly without a clue as to the relative greatness of the persons of the Godhead. Thus this claim displays graciousness on Jesus' part, consistent with his prior claim they would not be left orphans, comfortless, unempowered, but initiated into mysteries never before proclaimed. Notice that before Jesus no one ever spoke of Father, Son, Holy Spirit. The fact that Jesus did not use these terms didactically is again consistent with his claim of being one of those persons.
I have told you before it comes to pass	14-29	This claim stresses, not the fact that he was able to predict the future—by now this was commonplace—but he tells them what they would feel when it did come to pass...again, a gentle, kind reassurance that would remind them exactly of Jesus' manner while with them when it came to pass.
...the ruler of the world comes, and in me he has nothing [*he will indeed find nothing in me to enable him to gain power over me*—Cassirer]	14-30	This claim constitutes the formal diplomatic announcement of the end of Satan's tenure on the earth. Thus it was both a claim and more, a gauntlet thrown down in the face of the heavenly host, all of them: the four living creatures, watchers, seraphim, cherubim, principalities, powers, archons, thrones, lords, angels elect and fallen, demons, gods and God. Said at this time in this way, it is Jesus' announcement that the beach head had been secured, the enemy demilitarized and the world readied for turn-back to Eden's Maker after four thousand years of secession to a strange lord and a false god. It is the final answer to the colloquy in Job between the adversary and God, or the giant's challenge "give me a man, a male, an *ish,* [and I will overcome him]." Uttered without fanfare before eleven *Ish* in an upper room, the spiritual world undoubtedly heard it as a trumpet blast.

...but that the world may know that I love the Father, and as the Father has commanded me, thus I do.	14-31	*Still, what has to be accomplished is this, that the world is to come to know that I love the Father, and that the commandment laid down for me by the Father is the very thing I do* (Cassirer trans). Consider, these are Jesus' summary, parting words to his chosen disciples on his last night on earth, a fact of which he was conscious. We are all familiar with famous last words of fathers, soldiers, explorers, inventors, kings and falsely accused friends. Jesus' words are so different, so unique! Did ever a man utter words like this? "I have known from a child what my mission on earth is, I have kept to that mission and a final element demands the present and future world realize a man has been here who only acted on account of love, respect and obedience to God the Father." He waits for no reaction to these surely-not-understood words, but brings closure by adding "Well then, rise up and let us depart from here." What we are witnessing here is a claim that stymied heaven's created host, and on earth quelled every tongue of the creature bearing God's image and likeness.
I am the true vine...	15-1	This claim can only be appreciated in its historical context. Scriptures known to every simple or learned Jew from Sabbath outreadings compared their nation to a vine. *For the vineyard of Jehovah of hosts is the house of Israel* (Isaiah 5) *And I—I had planted thee a noble vine* (Jer. 2). So in this claim Jesus does not say *a vine* or *the vine* but the *true* vine in stark contrast to the nation of Israel that failed to bring forth good grapes. Jehovah had warned of cropping and pruning in such an event. Jesus identifies himself at this juncture as the replacement of the vine of Israel that his Father the husbandman was uprooting (see Eze 17:9-10) to replace with the man Jesus and his "branches," common earthy uneducated men who would sit on twelve thrones judging the twelve tribes of Israel.

...and my Father is the husbandman.	15-1	By this claim of heavenly knowledge, Jesus declares that the Father he has been introducing and speaking about is Jehovah of Hosts. The idea of Jehovah as a kind, concerned father inviting intimacy was brand spanking new. Scattered scriptural references — mostly metaphor, simile or adjective there were — both in Torah and writings of the prophets and psalmists. But to actually refer to that austere Jehovah God as a farmer, a worker, a vinegrower and then "my Father..." well, the sheer newness and boldness would have been breath-taking to Jesus' hearers. Imagine someone going on about the long line of distinguished diplomats and ambassadors waiting in line to get a ten minute audience with King Solomon, then concluding with "he's really a nice guy and would be delighted to have coffee with you, shall we stroll over now?"
I am the vine, ye are the branches.	15-5	Unlike his previous claim to be the *true* vine in contrast with the appointed but unfaithful nation, here Jesus is asserting simple precedence. Branches don't bear vines; vines bear branches. Lest disciples make the same mistake the nation had, Jesus states this claim emphatically, stressing consequences that even a child can understand.
Every branch... ...they are burned	15-2 to 6	Verses two thru six speak metaphorically of bearing fruit, purging, taking away, casting away, drying up, burning up, being clean by word, abiding—concepts that require understanding the metaphor. Readers and commentators find varying meanings so I won't add to the unraveling effort, leaving untouched what could well be iterated here as more claims by Jesus in this section.

...ye shall ask (*aiteo*) what ye will and it shall come to pass to you.	15-7	Not metaphor or hyperbole but a simple statement of fact from the only man qualified to make it without a "thus saith the Lord." Implicit in this assertion are all the factors that must be in place for such a broad, unlimited ability to be put in place. Consider: childish wishes, rebellion, God-like wishes, wishes monstrous to microscopic, creative to merely cosmetic, time independent, space-independent, natural-law-flaunting...where is *ask what ye will* bounded? These are surely underlying factors that had to be considered and weighed prior to Jesus deciding on the scope of power he was granting to his followers.
As the Father has loved me, I also have loved you: abide in my love.	15-9	Building on the claim of son/father relation Jesus enjoyed with God the Father, he claims absolutely what for another man would be wishful thinking: that the perfect, unimprovable love the Father displays toward Jesus is no greater and no less than what Jesus had displayed toward his disciples! John the writer and recipient shows in chapter 13:1 that he was persuaded of this. If your spouse says to you "in all my actions as well as in my heart I have perfectly loved you," you might recall times when that heartfelt affection was compromised by some trifling sharp reply or impatient response. No such recollection is recorded as coming from any of the twelve's most prolific writers, or even sound bites from those who have left us no writings.

This is my commandment, that ye love one another, as I have loved you.	15-12	A commandment is a tacit claim of authority. At the very least Jesus here presumes on the authority that comes from respect and gratitude. Having just said that his love was equal to the Father's, he now commands them to love one another with that same species of love. If such love were not possible, this would be mockery of the disciples. But no, he lays it on them as something he expects and will doubtless give them enablement to accomplish. Had he perhaps made a claim before coming to earth as to what he would accomplish here, of which this enablement is one item? This query will arise again shortly when we look at the ambassador's debriefing in chapter 17. [Observe: it is becoming apparent by now that Jesus is crafting a new race using a new image (Col 3); fully human like himself, but possessed of divine abilities and partakers of the divine nature. The ability to love occupies a distinct primacy in that roster of abilities. No creature up to the present has been able to abide in such a relationship or learn to use unselfishly such powers. Recall Jesus' words in Matthew: *and on this rock I will build my company [ecclesia]*. We are observing the laying of the collective foundation here on a rock footer, secure against the gates of hades as well as the winds and storms and floods of earth.]

...all things which I have heard of my Father I have made known to you.	15-15	Why is this a claim, rather than just a simple statement of fact? Because of the magnitude of what he is saying. Consider, a messenger holding back nothing—not merely delivering the message, but the tone, the innuendoes, the back and forth clarifications, hidden implications never divulged. Jesus is delivering a claim of imparting the ultimate knowledge contained in the spiritual world. He tells ordinary men intimate secrets shared by Diety in private counsel. Words fail me as I try to contrast the ethos and pathos, the sheer contrast between the spiritual import of words of a man who was and is and showed us God...and the ordinariness of the man Jesus.
...I have chosen you and I have set you that ye should go and ye should bear fruit...	15-16	This claim nestles in the section that opens up fruit-bearing, the precise thing that Adam and his descendents were hindered from accomplishing since ability to respond was lost at the fall. Jesus had come from God seeking fruit from men but found none. It was incumbent on him to reestablish fruit-bearing (15:12 above), and his claim here is that he has done so by *choosing* and *setting* these disciples. I repeat, these ordinary-sounding words acquire the sense of cosmic claims when Jesus' deity is admitted. If you bring strange new human powers to a race of ants you have transformed yourself to join, words descriptive of those powers will only be understood by those who admit your other-worldly origins. The ants who refuse to receive you as a former human will see your claims as nonsense. Think about those you know who dismiss John's gospel as ununderstandable nonsense, and you'll get the picture.
...that your fruit should abide...	15-16	Is this simply an expressed wish or is it a claim?
...that whatsoever ye shall ask the Father in my name he will give you.	15-16	A repeated claim that the Father would give on being asked, which obviously claims for Jesus an intimate knowledge and close association with the Father so as to speak and promise on His behalf.

If I had not come and spoken to them, they had not had sin...	**15-22**	When Al Gore volunteered that but for his assistance in its invention the Internet would not be here, we smiled at his boastfulness. Jesus is here claiming something bigger on a cosmic scale: that until there was extant in the world a life lived for Him and words faithfully declared, God would not judge men for their ignorance. Jesus is here claiming to have spoken and done perfectly, doings that were a final and convicting judgment of the world of men. The obvious corollary is that no other man since Adam had ever attracted God's eye and rewarding hand by doing what Jesus claims here to have done. When Satan said I will be like the Most High his words were noted, he was given room to pursue them, and they will be remembered again at his final sentencing—while God points to Jesus. God likes to point to an obscure or forgotten instance when judging, and say "look what the Ninevites did when Jonah addressed them," or "have you done what the queen of Sheba did when she learned of the existence of Solomon?" Western society likes this kind of thing as well, building it into our legal system under the rubric of *jury of one's peers*.

...but now they have no excuse for their sin.	15-22	A very solemn claim, and spoken in the hearing of God who will judge men including Jesus by their words. Jesus is saying here that his accomplishment cleared the way for God's scuttling the first Adam's entire race. Look at it as giving God Himself a choice: Adam or Jesus. Jesus had said (12:31) *now is the judgment of the world* referring to his life lived. While Jesus did not come to judge the world anymore than the Rechabites abstained from wine to condemn Israel (Jer 35), inevitably his life and words formed a basis upon which God's preference, and God's judgment alone can proceed. Let's bring this into modern times. If you are trying to make a point verbally like the African youth who insisted that warm water freezes faster than cold, or that bumblebees can indeed fly, the best way to communicate that fact is to simply point to the tray of ice cubes or the buzzing insect flying at 20 mph. Jesus points here to his life lived. Words spoken demand actions correspondent.
If I had not done among them the works which no other one has done, they had not had sin...	15-24	Not merely a repetition of the claim in verse 22 regarding his *words,* this claim by Jesus arrays his *works* on a level with his words—a bold assertion that his words and works could be superimposed without overlap—and offers disciples in this upper room what he will shortly refuse to give the high priestly Annas: testimony of his uniqueness. Caiaphas' sanhedrin would twist and use his adjured response that he was the son of the Blessed, as though he had spoken it from himself. (Yes, the ancient Jewish sanhedrin laid the groundwork of America's fifth amendment barring self-incrimination!) Nothing remains to be proven when a court finds words and actions in harmony. The claim of Jesus, "works no other one has done" stands unrefuted. The consequences do as well: those who refuse Jesus' words and works — leaders and followers alike — no longer will be deemed guiltless, *your sin* Jesus says, *remains.*(see 9:41)

...but now they have both seen and hated both me and my Father.	15-24	Moses could have said like words after Sinai's transgression: *now they have seen Jehovah descend on the mountain, heard His words and despised both in favor of a four-footed calf.* Just like Jesus, Moses had introduced God more intimately and with an unfamiliar name *Jehovah,* as Jesus had the *Father.* Just like Jesus, Moses' words demanded proof and Moses complied, working signs and wonders. Just like Jesus, Moses testified at the end of his mission *ye have been rebellious against Jehovah from the day that I knew you,* as Jesus in this claim. Saying they *hated both me and my Father* is first a claim of correctly judging their motives and second, that they could be said to have seen the Father merely by observing Jesus. Further, if Jesus had acceded to their request (chap 8) "where is this father of yours?" by showing them a spirit, they would have responded "you're using sorcery to trick us, show us something we can touch." Anticipating this, Jesus first showed them the Father in acts of human kindness, forgiveness, love and then spoke of Him. The nation's leadership refused both, inciting the wavering crowd to join in their hateful "Crucify!"

But that the word written in their law might be fulfilled, they hated me without a cause.	**15-25**	Here he says that David's words (see Psalm 69) were really a direct prophecy about himself, Jesus. A claim like this was not common among the Jewish leadership: the person making it would immediately be watched for any invalidating slip-up. Jesus, aware of this, throws down the gauntlet by saying "which of you convinces me of sin?" as though to say "you have been watching me for several years now. Testify!" Note as well again the expression "their law," not "our law" or even "the law." As we observed earlier, this is a tacit claim of not being under the law as they were, leaving one of two implications: the speaker was a foreigner or, if Jewish, the Messiah himself.

Reflection at this point: Perfection is possible to man; Jesus' demonstration of this changed everything. Post-Jesus, every human not able to do as he had done could not hold his head up before God—sinning had been shown to be unnecessary to man made in the image of God! Champions defeated, the hopes of those who would approach God on their own merits dissolve like smoke. But Israel's leaders were the champions of the human race and the discovery of fatal weakness not merely in that most favored nation but in humanity itself was more than disconcerting—it signaled moral necessity for a whole new race. Without this understanding in place, the good news of the gospel finds no audience.

But when the Comforter is come, whom I will send to you from the Father...	**15-26**	Clearly, by the ordinary, artless manner in which this claim was spoken, Jesus imagined himself sending from his native environment, heaven itself, near to God and His surroundings. In a previous claim (verse 26) he had spoken of the *Father* sending the Spirit, but visualizing that scene now he speaks of *personally* sending the comforting Spirit. While I am only listing verbal claims made by Jesus, a long roster of action-claims could serve as well. The manner in which Jesus makes this verbal claim forms an ancillary claim of comfort with heaven's surroundings that is not the contrived, ill-imagined lucubration of an inflated imagination but a reference to where he expected to be in forty days. Recall again Mark Twain's *The Prince and the Pauper* where Prince Edward describes his courtly upbringing. Pauper Tom would fall flat attempting to flesh out a single detail. A man claiming to describe a heaven he has not seen would be cautious of details that might expose him. Not so Jesus. His claims display a seamless consistency.
...*he* shall bear witness concerning me...	**15-26**	Another in this long list of testable claims. If I tell you that at my departure a stranger will appear and bear irrefutable evidence of my sayings including those you may have forgotten—your expectation would be set to meet the person. Jesus does that here. The Spirit of whose personhood they were not even sure—they knew only that God's *power* was vested in the "Spirit" of OT writings—is described by Jesus here in great detail. This is a claim of knowing where to find Him, securing the Father's agreement to send Him, and telling Him precisely what He should do when come. And yes, tested for almost two thousand years, this claim has stood up. Ask any of Jesus' disciples!

They shall 1) put you out of the synagogues; 2)...every one who kills you will think to render service to God.	**16-1** (2)	Unlike the well-known pagan oracles then extant, note how crisp and uncluttered by ambiguity Jesus' predictions are! Contrast a Nostradamus whose sayings can only be given credulity in retrospect. Example: *"The young lion will overcome the older one, On the field of combat in a single battle; He will pierce his eyes through a golden cage, Two wounds made one, then he dies a cruel death."* When Jesus speaks of coming things, his claims have the same tone as his other words, unshrouded by mystery. The imagery is that of a participant rather than an observer from a far vantage place, unacquainted with the vissisitudes of the actual combat or even identities of the combatants: by contrast, "young lion" and "older one" are suggestive of just such a limited view.
...these things they will do because they have not known the Father nor me.	**16-3**	Not only does Jesus speak specifically, but he also uses the broad strokes of a historian commenting on the motivation behind the recorded acts. This claim is clearly the language of a writer offering his conclusions from observations rather than a soldier describing a hand-to-hand conflict. Not many seers in human history have dared to do this.

But now I go to him that has sent me	16-5	Jesus speaks of going back to heaven with the casualness of "let's move into the living room." But by saying *to him that sent me* rather than "to heaven" he is gently acclimating them to new language they will shortly be using on his departure. If I say "I'm going to heaven," you would hear it as a boast that I am doing what other men cannot; If I say I'm returning to my boss you would hear it as something you can easily identify with, having a boss yourself. But if I say I'm returning to the one that sent me, your attention gets fixed on who that may be. So in this claim Jesus is forging links between his disciples and the God and Father they would shortly come to know. This reiterates the claim to Nicodemus that Jesus would take with him into the heavens, the manhood he had assumed. God's son came from the heavens. God's son returned to the heavens as son of man in a human body, the only such body presently there. That heaven-shaking event couched in this simply-worded claim belies the magnitude of the appearance of a man in a body of flesh and bones in heaven itself.

Pause here and note. The intrusion of an earthly man into the spiritual heavens is an event that was, I believe, largely unanticipated by heaven's host. Spiritual protocol and custom surely precluded the thought that a mortal, temporal, flesh and blood being could enter heaven and live. Angelic messengers from God to men on earth found them "a little lower," possessed of but rudimentary power, subject to time and vicissitude including death (a separation of spirit and body unknown there), and under the ban of banishment from their original dwelling in the garden of God. The distinction between heaven and earth's inhabitants could scarcely be greater. Hints that a radical shift of creature power was in the offing, were there. Witness the various openings of the heavens to men like Moses, Daniel, Ezekiel, Isaiah...each spoke of seeing a "son of man-like" being. But hints are not details. Add to this lack of details a major detail: the book whose topic sentence is left dangling with one half the subject untouched: *God created the **heavens and the earth*** is followed in the next sixty nine books by *and **the earth** was*...we expect to read somewhere the parallel expression *and **the heavens**...*followed by sixty-nine like books about heaven, but searching Genesis to Revelation there is no such statement and development, only occasional hints like, *the heavens are unclean in his sight, Behold I create new heavens and a new earth, Oh that you would tear the heavens, Hear O heaven and give ear O earth!, what is man that you are mindful of him?* ...all hints to readers that the history of the heavens was not completed and written up...why not? Until the heavens were opened to and occupied by a son of man, the mystery of God could not be revealed. The heavens and the earth carried separate histories until that moral juncture. There simply was no way that the eleven disciples upon hearing Jesus say "now I go to him that sent me," could have any inkling of what that arrival would do to the heavenlies. John was so unprepared as an old man on Patmos that when he saw Jesus arrayed in heavenly garb he dropped over as dead.

CLAIM	Chap Verse	COMMENT
But I say the truth to you, it is profitable for you that I go away; for if I do not go away, the Comforter will not come to you; but if I go I will send him to you.	16-7 (2)	Two claims here. The first appears to acknowledge an unknown protocol of heaven requiring the ambassador to return ere another one be sent. The second claim reiterates Jesus' previous claim that having arrived in heaven, his reception would be such that authority would be granted a man (!) entering the heavenly surroundings to ask a Person of the Godhead to go to earth to continue Jesus' own mission. It puts one in mind of the singularity enjoyed by Joshua on the day of the sun standing still "And there was no day like that before it or after it, that Jehovah hearkened to the voice of a man." Or the words spoken to Jacob, "you have wrestled with God and with men and have prevailed." Or Daniel, to whom it was almost wistfully confided by a high ranking angelic being: "<u>you</u> are a man greatly beloved,"—an expression not used in reference to angels. It might be well to comment as an overarching sidenote here, that if the heavens and the earth are to conjoin in the person of the man Jesus, he would surely be instructing both the heavenly beings and earthly beings in the new protocols that will obtain when heaven and earth are conjoined as they never were from their creation. Jesus knew clearly (see comments on 13:1 and 13:3, *Jesus knowing*) where he came from and where he was going. If you are a Mom or Dad taking your children back to a haunt of your childhood, you will surely be instructing them along the way, what they may encounter and how to meet it. Jesus is doing this here with both disciples and the constantly-watching angels.

And having come, he will bring demonstration to the world of sin, of righteousness, and of judgment.	16-8	More specifics in this claim of foretelling exactly what the Spirit will do. But a tacit claim is that he will be acting not from himself but on what he hears...from whom? Jesus. So not only does a man send a person of the Godhead (see prev. comment) but directs him precisely what to say, a claim no man dare make. It is clear from this claim that Jesus visualizes himself in charge once arrived in heaven, just as Joseph visualized himself in charge of Egypt as he advised Pharoah what to do. *Note*. It is becoming more difficult to catalog these advanced claims since they can only be grasped upon accepting Jesus' previous claims. Thus as we go deeper into this structured hierarchy, they become progressively the possession of attentive, believing readers. Such exoteric/esoteric structuring runs thru scripture: *more shall be given,* Jesus says *to him that hath.* While I won't repeat this observation, you will need to recall it when claims you read here become obtuse: the fault lies not with how scripture presents them but in how you and I expect to receive them. Most readers just ignore and overleap these "claims" as not claims at all.

...I go away to my Father...	**16-10**	A frequent claim by now, reiterated here in a natural, conversational tone without attempting to impress by words emphasizing the claim's magnitude. Jesus was showing by examples like this, how the Father is pleased by His creatures' manner of speaking, and this mannerism was quickly taken up by Jesus' disciples. Speaking of his experiencing the third heaven, Paul refers (2 Cor 12) to "a man in Christ" rather than "me." Speaking dispassionately—while not without passion when needed—has become one hallmark of Jesus' followers. Extravagance and verbal embellishment are hallmarks of deceivers —if you know what you are saying is true, you're don't need to puff it up with adjectives. That Paul had learned this is quite evident from passages like 10:14 *For we do not, as not reaching to you, overstretch ourselves...*a striking contrast to the false teachers rampant in his absense, whose bombastic boasting Paul points to repeatedly.
...the ruler of this world is judged.	**16-11**	Earlier, Jesus identifies the ruler of the world as Satan (see 14-30) which makes this a reference to a judgment taking place in the heavenlies rather than on earth—quite a statement for a man on earth to make! Another claim emerges from the simple pronoun ***this*** *[world]* rather than ***the*** *[world]* as in 14-30. There must be another world if ours is referenced as *this world.* So Jesus is claiming the demise of the present world in the condign judgment of its ruler. We'll find a related, corroborating claim in the last verse of our chapter, where Jesus will claim to have vanquished the world.

I have many things to say to you but ye cannot bear them now.	16-12	Read quickly without thinking, you see just a simple statement. But for anyone believing Jesus' words this is a claim—that he had many more heavenly things to relate which he was holding in abeyance to relate later. Ask any believer in Jesus whether they have experienced the truth of this claim and you'll get a resounding *yes!* We actually have far more understanding of Jesus' person and works than his disciples did while with him! Any of the apostles would agree that what they received *after Jesus' life and ministry ended* exceeded what they had when with him for the three-odd years called "the days of his [Jesus'] flesh." Thus the epistles are replete with the things Jesus is here speaking of as unable to be communicated while he was, and the Spirit was not, *dwelling* on earth (and also, by the way, why those who search for "the historical Jesus" to find childhood and parental factors that made him what he was are always disappointed—they only connect with (a tiny portion of) his life here on earth, totally missing the essentials!)
But when *he* is come, the Spirit of truth...	16-13	See 14:17 where Jesus first uses this name for the Spirit. Thus two claimshere. First, the Spirit would come in the near future. Second, what the Spirit of truth would do. (see following claim)
...he shall guide you into all the truth...	16-13	Once again, a powerful "all," indicative of what Jesus has in mind for his followers. While Jesus' disciples over the past two thousand years have been experiencing the reality of this claim, they will tell you at once that the depths they have plumbed are only scratching the surface. And note the language: *guide you* is quite different from channel (see 8:28 and 12:50) implant or dump on you; it supposes a process that is yet ongoing and will continue as the Spirit works in fellowship with those He indwells.

...for he shall not speak from himself; but whatsoever he shall hear he shall speak...	**16-13**	And now, the reason for the above claim: it is *for he shall not speak from himself [as source]* but will be declaring what Jesus had to hold in abeyance (see 16:12 above). Thus this is another claim of Jesus to be on a level with the Spirit as well as the Father, a claim no other dare make. Jesus, a man, is telling them what, why, and how the Spirit of God will act in the future! A man, Jesus, will give Him words. Recall God's rebuke to a high-ranking man, Job, for daring to speak inadvisedly to and of God. (Job 40:2). This is clearly a claim by Jesus to be on equality with God.
...and he will announce to you what is coming.	**16-13**	Jesus' claim here is that not only will he provide for his disciples in his absence ("not leave you orphans" above), but goes into specific claims of what they can expect. This claim tells them that unlike ordinary men they will have an unerring knowledge of what to expect as it comes on the world and on them while they are yet in a world they are not "of." If you had your choice of taking the word of a psychic, a historian, a Wall Street analyst, a politician or a professional futurist, would you take any of these in preference to Jesus?

He shall glorify me...	16-14	We humans seek our own glory; Persons of the Godhead never do, instead Father and Son and Spirit glorify each other. This claim that he would be glorified by the Spirit, already begun and already verified by Jesus' followers, advances the agenda mentioned above that Jesus is shutting down the no-more-useful Adam race and starting anew as the Second man, the Last Adam. Again, these details of Earth's coming race of men are unintelligible to those who do not buy in to Jesus' claim, and since typical human conversation rarely uses expressions like these, Jesus' words here are deemed weird, unmeaningful by all such deniers. Imagine listening to a world famous composer going on rapturously about a Bach fugue —to a kindergarten class. Get the idea? When Jesus says *he shall glorify me* he's speaking of happenings as normal in the spiritual world as combing our hair or walking down the street here. An angel understands this at once; we kindergarteners only by the effort of mentally transporting ourselves into a realm of doings wildly unknown here. Singling out excellence in others and celebrating it is what beings near God do. All day. Every day. Contrast humans' fixation on finding faults and celebrating them, seizing good and gulping it, purity and sullying it...this is why Jesus' words and claims here are so difficult for us! By accepting claims such as this one, we're weaned away from Adam's ways to espouse Jesus!
...he shall receive of mine and shall announce it to you.	16-14	If a stranger at a restaurant counter engages me in conversation, telling me he's come into a fabulous fortune in a third-world country and a specially chosen curator there will shortly begin cataloging their value and sending notice of shipment to the guests dining with us I'd be skeptical. Here we have Jesus, a man about to die shamefully, speaking of treasures in heaven that are his and will be shared shortly upon his absence. Has this claim come true? Ask his followers.

All things that the Father has are mine...	16-15	Could a human being make a more extravagant claim than this? While our cosmic peers—angelics and the host—would hear this statement even more extravagantly than we, Jesus spoke it to men who like Manoah, Samson's clueless father, were as ignorant of spiritual matters as they were intrigued by them. Jesus spoke these precise words for this precise audience, so we need not back away from his statement. One of the clearest messages that comes thru to unspiritual hearers is nearness between Father and Son. Another that follows hot on its heels is wonderment about what one can name that the Father (Whom we do not know apart from what Jesus tells us) "has." At first blush it is a difficult conception since we humans are so used to equating having with physical possessions—hardly applicable to spirit, unless by taking literally verses like *every beast of the forest is mine, the cattle upon a thousand hills...if I were hungry I would not tell thee; for the world is mine, and the fulness thereof. (Ps 50)*. Spoken by Jesus to men, in the sight of the heavenly host, this claim of Jesus is unlike any that another man would make...I can think of nothing to compare to it.
...on account of this I have said he receives of mine and announces [it] to you.	16-15	More than a repetition of the above, Jesus notes that saying *receive of mine* might not convey anything concrete and so kindly adds that *mine* includes *all things that the Father has*, making the store of things infinite. The Spirit can thus draw from anything the Son has, which includes all that the Father has, making me ask here "What does that NOT include?"

A little (Gr. *micros*) and ye do not behold me, and again a little and ye shall see me.	16-16	A repetition of 14:19, 28; 16:5, 7, 10 where he establishes he will be gone, they will "see" him while the world will not, he is returning to his sender, his comings and goings are to and from the Father...here he adds to the litany that it will be quicker than they think: a *little while,* full well expecting they will choke on that *micro.* When one makes understandable claims one uses everyday language. Making claims of unfamiliar things demands novel language and locutions. We might never considered these words of Jesus as claims, since they differ so strikingly from typical human claims. In speaking of the unfamiliar one seeks a reference point in the familiar to hang the new thing on for connection. This becomes difficult when everything is new, describing a whole 'nother world as Jesus is doing here. Note well Jesus' methods of bridging the spiritual/carnal gap with ordinary disciples... hardly what one expects from an unlettered Galilean.
...I will see you again, and your heart shall rejoice, and your joy no one takes from you.	16-22	The reunion Jesus here announces is what the disciples would be longing for, at least those who believed that Jesus was not long for this world. Thomas had already said *Let us also go, that we may die with him* so there was a measure of expectation among them that Jesus might die, as they well knew from the plotting rulers. Instead of explaining how he would die, be buried, rise again, spend portions of forty days with them, ascend, be honored in heaven, and ask to send the Spirit with things from the Father and Son in heaven that would lead to the joy of reunion—Jesus makes a single claim that cuts to the chase. "I will see you again." This, to prepare them for the unbelievable: A dead man rising. Claims like this speak more to the heart than the mind, and Jesus knows it. Those of us who have had loving mothers and fathers often had to be satisfied with just such a comforting word when explanations would have left us confused.

Whatsoever ye shall ask the Father he will give you in my name.	16-23	Imagine your third grade companion is the son of the US president, and his incurable illness will take him from you in a week. He says, *Mention my name—my Dad will give you whatever you ask!* Would you dare ask? Jesus, the ambassador from heaven extends eleven disciples an unbelievable boon—direct access to heaven and Him who sits on the throne. Did they "get it?" No. But four sentences later it began to penetrate: *Now you speak plainly!*
...ask, and ye shall receive, that your joy may be full.	16-24	By now a familiar exhortation: *Ask.* Jesus' claims have consitently been putting forth varied reasons and consequences of asking. Presented to the disciples as commands, claims like this presuppose Jesus is an ambassador of heaven, authorized to extend high privileges to men on earth.
...the Father himself has affection for you, because you have had affection for me...	16-27	When you introduce me to your employer, or your PR agent or even an old friend, you might say "Harvey, my friend Robert has been itching to meet you ever since he heard of the special working relation you and I enjoy." Here is Jesus doing the same for disciples. Isn't it a pleasure to meet someone who has been looking forward to making your acquaintance? God the Father is anxious to meet *me?*
I came out from-with (para w/ genitive) God.	16-27	This claim read in the original language suggests coming out from immediate, intimate presence, and is so used in this gospel. Jesus is not part of a group or contingent but the personal messenger of God Himself, in this claim. The only other man said to come "from with" God is the baptiser, John, the greatest of those born of women. (1:6)

I came out from the Father and have come into the world; again, I leave the world and go to the Father.	**16-28** (4)	Four claims intimately subjoined. When we hear someone say "I'm leaving the world," we presume he's talking about death, quite unlike Jesus here. When Jesus speaks of coming into the world, it's not so much human birth as the whole process of incarnation of a spiritual being, as well as it's reverse "I leave the world and go to the Father"...spoken like we'd say "I'm going into the living room." Since both of these actions—coming and going—are unprecedented in our experience we are forced to take Jesus' words at face value and wait to find out exactly what it means for a spirit to enter manhood and for a man to return to spiritual surroundings in his human body. Claims like these four become incendiary to disciples, especially when linked to other claims like *I will come again and receive you unto myself, that where I am ye also may be.*
...ye shall be scattered, each to his own, and shall leave me alone; and [yet] I am not alone, for the Father is with me.	**16-32**	This claim, that the Father would be with him even when all his disciples had run away, is an invitation to Jesus' followers to believe what seems to contradict: *My God, why have you abandoned me?* Since I'm enumerating claims here and not commenting doctrinally, I will only mention that nowhere are the Father and God more distinguished as well as more co-identified than in John's writings. Apparent contradictions are often inlets to things previously unknowable, and placed there precisely to generate a "pause and consider" notice—thoughtful kindnesses from the author.

I have conquered the world.	16-33	Other conquerors have made a similar claim. One of them, Napoleon, had this to say: "Alexander, Caesar, Charlemagne and I myself have founded great empires; but upon what did these creations of our genius depend? Upon force. Jesus alone founded His empire upon love, and to this very day millions will die for Him...I think I understand something of human nature; and I tell you, all these were men, and I am a man; none else is like Him: Jesus Christ was more than a man...I have inspired multitudes with such an enthusiastic devotion that they would have died for me...but to do this it was necessary that I should be visibly present with the electric influence of my looks, my words, of my voice. When I saw men and spoke to them, I lightened up the flame of self-devotion in their hearts...Christ alone has succeeded in so raising the mind of man toward the unseen, that it becomes insensible to the barriers of time and space." And note this corroboration comes seventeen centuries after Jesus' claim.
Father, the hour has come...	17-1	**I'll leave unenumerated the fifty or more claims in this chapter.** My object is to list claims made by Jesus to men, be they public or, as in the last four chapters, more private to his own disciples...private that is, as distinguished from secret (*in secret I have spoken nothing* 18:30). The fifty-odd 'claims' in this chapter appear to be part of a debriefing—an ambassador's "Mission Accomplished" report. Spoken to the Father who sent him, these hardly qualify as claims made before men.
I am he.	18-5 & 8	Not a claim contested or misunderstood by the hearers, and not a claim of more than ordinary signification. I list it here merely as background to the more extravagant claims, showing that the ordinary man who acknowledged being Jesus of Nazareth is the same person who asserted the claims of being more than a mere man.

...the cup which my Father has given me...	**18-11**	A tacit claim that resolves what is left ambiguous by the other gospel writers: Was Jesus' request to the Father merely answered by silence as a reader can conclude from Matthew, Mark and Luke's account, or answered in the negative? By speaking these words in response to Peter's insistence by word and sword that this "not happen" to him, Jesus is clearly claiming that a "cup"—acceptance of rejection, violence and death at the hands of men—was indeed there for him to take if he would. He did.
...in secret I have spoken nothing.	**18-20**	A simple claim that unlike his contemporaries (conspirators like Theudas, Judas the Galilean and Barabbas) Jesus had not covertly planned, taught, or instigated an agenda against the Jewish administration other than the plain words with which he had publicly spoken against them and their practices. This claim doubtless would have brought to his hearer's minds similar sayings by all the prophets.
My kingdom is not of this world...my kingdom is not from hence.	**18-36**	Note that in making this claim before Pilate, Jesus does not stray from his announced, acknowledged identity as Sent One from God and fellow-grantee of authority such as Pilate was exercising. Other men would be cowed before Pilate, thus this is another instance of *consistency of actions with exotic claims* we've been noticing throughout John's narrative. To paraphrase, *While I have a kingdom, it is of a kind that has no overlap with yours.*

Thou sayest, that I am a king. I have been born for this, and for this I have come into the world, that I might bear witness to the truth.	**18-37**	Very careful language here, for very important reasons. By placing emphasis on *thou* Jesus is reminding him that Pilate is quoting others who have accused him, rather than Jesus who, unlike the rabble-rousers were self-proclaimers. Pilate is a judge. Jesus appeals saying (paraphrasing): *You are asking whether I am challenging your authority by proclaiming myself to be king, a charge others have accused me of and you are repeating. But there is a prior claim that demands hearing and I will make it: I am here to bear witness to the truth.* He had earlier asked if the accusation was being made by Pilate himself, or if it was an accusation of hearsay, which would make a great deal of difference, a difference that Pilate was attempting to gloss over. For Jesus to affirm kingship in the world governed by Roman officials such as Pilate was treason, punishable as such. While Jesus regarded himself as rightful king it was never his custom to proclaim it, evidenced for example by sayings like, "Jerusalem...the city of the great king," rather than "Jerusalem, my royal residence." So the leaders here were forced to say that Jesus "makes himself king" rather than quoting his words that he was their king...there were no such words to quote and Pilate would have adjudged that a false charge. My reason for including this as a claim is the fact that Jesus never denied being a king, while carefully avoiding traps to use self-proclaimed kingship against him. In this case the effort of Jewish leaders to use Jesus' obvious kingship to persuade Pilate to find Jesus guilty, actually boomeranged as by that act they formally dissociated themselves from God's anointed Messiah (see Ps 2:6-7) in favor of Caesar as their king.

I have been born for this, and for this I have come into the world, that I might bear witness to the truth.	**18-37**	Several claims here, stated interestingly. Note the verbs *born* and *come*. Jesus uses both. Being born of a woman makes you a man. Being come indicates preexistence, unlike other men. Scripture nowhere refers to any man but Jesus as coming into the world. John the baptiser is said to have been sent 'from with' the Father, but not as having prior existence. (John's epistle chapter 4 takes this even farther as an confession of faith in Jesus as uniquely *come in flesh*). So what we have here is Jesus' uniqueness stated in this couplet. The one God sent to bear witness to the truth must be both familiar with heavenly as well as earthly—he must *come* and he must be *born*. Jesus claims here to be that one. Then he adds another claim asserting he knows why he is here (versus most men who fail to discover this in their lifetimes). He is here to witness to the truth. That supposes both ability and a commission.
Every one that is of the truth hears my voice.	**18-37**	There may well have been or be self-inflated men who would make a claim like this. Pilate's reaction shows he was not unfamiliar with discussions of truth, coming from an educated tradition that had begun to philosophically explore such concepts four centuries prior. Socrates, Plato and Aristotle all reasoned and wondered about truth. Examination of Jesus' use of the word truth exhibits a familiarity with truth, and a personal connection that is lacking in others: the fact that he generally referred to *the* truth rather than simply *truth* in the abstract as something unknowable sets Jesus' many claims about the truth apart (comparing Jesus' utterances with say, Plato in his *Republic*).

Woman, behold thy son... ...behold thy mother.	**19-26,27**	A claim of a high order, reminiscent of his changing a human relationship (Simon to Cephas) but with broader, racial significance. An ordinary man making such statements would mean "treat this person as you would your son/mother," — and Jesus certainly meant that personal, limited meaning — but since that day his followers have adopted this attitude wholesale to include the entire family of believers. And quite beyond even that, these two statements appear to build on what Jesus' death and resurrection would accomplish in the spiritual world, though a bit beyond the scope of my subject here.
I thirst.	**19-28**	We all say, "I'm thirsty." What makes this a claim? Motive. John supplies Jesus' motive for making this statement: *that the scripture might be fulfilled,* thus making this expression more than a simple feeling of thirst. Jesus was aware that *the things [written] concerning me have an end.* That is, that there was a precise set of scriptural statements he had undertaken to complete. It was written "in my thirst they gave me vinegar to drink." Such a statement cannot be fulfilled by an mere actor performing—and Jesus' thirst was not contrived or choreographed acting. The reality was what Jesus went thru; the scriptural description (David, Ps 69) was but a pointer, centuries earlier. Jesus claims here to be fulfilling the scriptures; in the next claim, that he did so completely and thoroughly, bringing an era (Gr. *aion*) to an end.
It is finished.	**19-30**	Among heavenly and earthly workers, doubtless the greatest claim ever made. Upon informing Adam that from the day of his trangression he and his had become workers of the ground, God donned workman's garb as well. Father and Son broke shabbat and began tending their earthly creation. (see 5:17) The steward appointed to till and guard God's garden found himself relegated to another role, that of waiting patiently until what he had failed to accomplish was finished by the woman's seed.

...folded up in a distinct place by itself.	**20-7**	I've been cataloging words, spoken words by Jesus that are claims. I can't resist adding an action here where no words were spoken. When you know someone is following you, leaving a clue replaces speech. A misplaced twig in a footprint, a scrap left carelessly or carefully on the trail, a false clue or "red herring" all are examples of details that signal your eyes as unusual words signal your ears: they emphasize a feature, arresting the observer's attention. In this case, the body wrappings lay intact, indicating the body somehow passed thru them. The napkin had been folded and carefully moved, indicating the folder (whether an angel or as I suspect, Jesus himself) was leaving a message that would be understood by someone diligent enough to show up at that juncture. The unspoken claim would then be: "Surprised that my words about rising have come to pass?" ...making this a claim that he was risen and active.
...I have not yet ascended to my Father...	**20-17**	Yet again a claim by Jesus of free access to the heavens of God as he had to the earth he had made. If you look up and see your husband coming from the gate with other coal miners you would doubtless wave, or if nearer, approach to greet—and be surprised by his put-off "Wait till I get home and wash up." Going to the Father's side was as natural for Jesus as going home is to a worker. Have you ever met a man who could as casually refer to heaven's furniture as to his own? Jesus' repeated talk of heaven, the angels, the Father, His house, His counsels, His solicitude both in heaven and with a sparrow on earth are *claims*, not rambling nonsense as unbelieving academics would have it.

I ascend to my Father and your Father, and [to] my God and your God.	**20-17**	Casual reading fails to detect a claim here, just a simple statement (and probably unbelievable as well). But note that consistent with his ambassadorial role, Jesus constantly builds on what he has formally declared, whether his hearers understood or not. It's evident that a change has taken place. Jesus for the first time references "my Father and your Father." The intimacy with the Father that up to his death and resurrection was unique to him, has now become shareable with Jesus' own. John is exquisitely precise in both his gospel and epistles distinguishing *the, my* and *your* Father. From this point on it became true that those believing on Jesus were brought into a visible family, able to say *Abba*, a familiar form of address by children, never a servant's privilege. Family customs, closely guarded in enduring cultures, often are chronicled in novels and biographies where after long association a stranger's allegiance finally inducts him or her into an inner circle, privileged to come and go as a child of the household. The turning point highlighted in this simple statement of Jesus was and could only be understood by one who had been treasuring Jesus' words. Mary of Magdala qualified herself and thus becomes the bringer of news awaited from the time of Adam and Eve's expulsion. The heir had come, restoring the relationship mankind's father and mother forfeited. As proof of that fact he informs her in words only the awaited one could give to the four-thousand-year waiters... *my Father and your Father* would become the new name by which the God of Eden is known.

...he breathed into [them] and says, Receive Holy Spirit...	20-22	This claim, that he was identifying and preparing the eleven for a long-promised event takes on significance in view of the buildup to it by the Jewish prophets Jeremiah, Ezekiel, Isaiah, Joel and others. I know of nothing in history on an array with this singular event. Humanity was changed fifty days later when, upon Jesus' ascent and reception in heaven the Spirit arrived to dwell in new surroundings—living bodies of men, purchased and claimed as His, jointly prepared by Jesus for *indwelling.* Note I am not speaking of a religious belief but an actual event in history whose effects are demonstrably felt to the present day. The bland phrase "Humanity was changed" above should read "Mankind's evolution leaped forward," but the mental hiccup might be explosive for traditional Bible-readers! I'll say only that the arrested development of our race underwent a supercharged, lasting change—a change accelerating the growth process stymied for four thousand years from Adam's expulsion to the Spirit's arrival.
...whosoever sins ye remit, they are remitted; whosoever ye retain, they are retained.	20-23	Try replacing that word *sins* with the equivalent *errings*...how does it sound now? Jesus had already claimed authority on earth to forgive errings. Now, about to return to heaven, protocol demands that unbroken succession be kept up on earth by duly recognized members of Heaven's kingdom. Without going into differences between judicial, governmental and administrative forgiveness, recognize merely that in this claim of ability to appoint successors, Jesus is once again in full compliance with both earthly and heavenly protocol. Sins against heaven demand heaven's authority to remit; here Jesus confers it.
Bring your finger here and see my hands; and bring your hand and put it in my side...	20-27	Clearly a claim by Jesus to be the same person resurrected that they had known for the past few years. Secondly, a claim of touchable corporeality and perhaps more since he invites Thomas to put his hand *in,* not merely "touch my side" as though examining a closed wound.

...blessed they who have not seen and have believed.	**20-29**	By saying "they" instead of "your fellow-disciples" Jesus, as ever, speaks words immediately understandable to the physical listeners, yet expandable without stretching to all of us who for twenty centuries have done like the ten rather than like Thomas. Thus this is a claim of God's blessing resting on all who subsequent to that occasion believe on an unseen Jesus—far better than 99.9% if you do the math: *10 disciples divided by XXX million disciples = just shy of 100%.*
Cast the net at the right side of the ship and you will find.	**21:6**	Fishermen, whether bait-and-hook or net-casters, try to predict where the catch will be when they begin to cast. Rarely are they successful—an entire industry has grown up today offering lures, advice, tips and sounding equipment, mostly to little avail. Jesus seems to know their feelings and more: unsolicited, he breaks their morose silence without even identifying himself. Note this is the last time Jesus tells a group or an individual fisherman exactly how to obtain a catch, making this a repeated claim with a high degree of success. In the cultural context of the Jewish disciples, withholding and multiplying or preparing fish was an often-referenced subject of prophecies, and that awareness surfaces here as John looks up, understanding dawns, and his sotto-voce to Peter *It is the Lord,* enlightens the shadowy figure on the shore as the source of the bulging net.

...when you are old, you will stretch forth your hands and another will lead you where you do not wish.	**21-18**	I've had a number of people—mother, teacher, friend—look at my youthful exuberance or sauciness and say "Harvey, when are grown up you will..." and in many cases they have been correct. So this claim of Jesus to be able to foresee the time and manner (with hands stretched forth, i.e. crucified) of Peter's chosen way of glorifying God was noted both by John, and by Peter as he says in his last letter: *the putting off of my tent is speedily to take place, as also our Lord Jesus Christ has manifested to me.* Thus the first and last claims of Jesus in John's account both concern Peter. The first was his renaming, and the last his enduring affection that would lead him to follow his master as he had desired *"I will lay down my life for you."*

CLOSING COMMENT

Solomon collected, pondered, composed and wrote.

Songs, proverbs, a song of songs, wisdom, reflections, advice, chronicles of labor under the sun – and a parting warning (preface p. 1) about endless making of books. His wisdom contrasts wordy activity with proper use of words: "acceptable, upright, words of truth."

Like Moses, David, Job, Isaiah and others, Solomon the wisest yielded the stage to another, a man yet to come.

Jesus was that man. He could say of Moses "he wrote of me." He could say "Abraham exulted to see my day." "David," Jesus said "calls [me] Lord." "Isaiah," John testifies, spoke "because he saw [Jesus'] glory." And the last of the prophets, greatest of those born of women, yielded to Jesus with the words "he must increase, but I must decrease."

Into the arena thus emptied of Adam, of patriarchs and of prophets, Jesus enters. His first recorded words in John's gospel are "What seek ye?"… precisely according to protocol; the answer to Adam's expulsion concluding four thousand years of waiting. Jesus takes center stage in the vacant arena, receiving two seekers with "Come and see." Archtypal words, no doubt.

"The words of the wise," Solomon intones, "are like goads, and the collections of them as nails fastened in."

Goaded by Jesus' words Andrew and Philip act. But the 'collecting' and 'fastening in' of Jesus' words was left to a disciple who leaned on Jesus' bosom.

John gives us words neither Matthew, Mark nor Luke dare to offer. Take for example, John's intimate explanation of what was going on inside

Jesus when he reports that Jesus "*knowing that his hour was come for him to depart out of this world to the father*...rises." The three evangelists give us bare facts and actions like "he rises." John dares tell us exactly why Jesus rose from supper, almost as though, his head over Jesus' heart, a channel had opened to his ear.

For two millennia Jesus' followers have witnessed an odd phenomenon. Words and phrases, isolatedly quoted from discourses of Jesus we acknowledgedly don't understand, prove useful day after day, goading us to act.

But the *collection* John has gathered and offers us in these several hundreds of claims still waits to see its day. My intuition and hope is that someone will connect the dots allowing a single figure to emerge.

www.ingramcontent.com/pod-product-compliance
Lightning Source LLC
Chambersburg PA
CBHW071736080526

44588CB00013B/2050